NEW DEVELOPMENTS IN MEDICAL RESEARCH

FLOW IN THE HEALTH SCIENCES FOR DISEASE PREVENTION AND HEALTH PROMOTION

NEW DEVELOPMENTS IN MEDICAL RESEARCH

Additional books in this series can be found on Nova's website under the Series tab.

Additional e-books in this series can be found on Nova's website under the e-book tab.

NEW DEVELOPMENTS IN MEDICAL RESEARCH

FLOW IN THE HEALTH SCIENCES FOR DISEASE PREVENTION AND HEALTH PROMOTION

KAZUKI HIRAO

New York

NOTICE TO THE READER

Library of Congress Cataloging-in-Publication Data

ISBN: 978-1-63482-763-8

Library of Congress Control Number: 2015940243

Published by Nova Science Publishers, Inc. † New York

Contents

Preface

Suffering from many years of pain, some people choose death over life. Reasons for this suffering are diverse and can include relationship problems, poverty or discrimination. In addition, depression is one of the most relevant mental illnesses that lead to suicidal tendencies. Depression is a very familiar disease. Furthermore, multiple genetic and environmental factors cause depression. People with depression will be unable to enjoy their daily life. On the other hand, some people continue through life filled with a sense of fulfillment. Such a person is not only interested in various things but is also actively involved in various activities. Where does this difference come from?

This book will examine quality of life in terms of flow, which is one's ability to become fully absorbed in something. Moreover, I hope this book will provide useful guidance to the readers.

Chapter 1

Flow

Abstract

This chapter first explains the definition of "flow" and outlines the conditions for "flow" to occur. I will then give a concrete example of the flow experience and argue for the potential use of "flow" in the health science domain. Finally, I introduce a method for measuring "flow".

Definition of Flow

Flow is defined as "the holistic sensation that people feel when they act with total involvement" [1]. Flow is also "the state in which people are so involved in an activity that nothing else seems to matter; the experience itself is so enjoyable that people will do it even at great cost, for the sheer sake of doing it" [2]. Not based on profit-and-loss considerations, such as whether a given action is useful at the moment, flow is the condition of feeling value in doing something at the moment. It is an intrinsically driven state. Flow has also been described as follows: "intense and focused concentration on what one is doing in the present moment," "[the] merging of action and awareness," "loss of reflective self-consciousness (i.e., loss of the awareness of oneself as a social actor)," "a sense that one can control one's actions; that is, a sense that one can in principle deal with the situation because one knows how to respond to whatever happens next," "distortion of temporal experience (typically, a sense that time has passed faster than normal)," "experience of the activity as intrinsically rewarding, such that often the end goal is just an excuse for the process" [3].

Flow is a state in which abilities are maximized. It occurs when one's challenge and skill levels are balanced. However, challenge and skill levels are not always balanced: When one's skill level exceeds one's challenge level, relaxation, then boredom, can result. In contrast, when one's challenge level exceeds one's skill level, uneasiness results. It is necessary to coordinate challenge and skill levels to avoid boredom and uneasiness.

Examples of the Flow Experience

Flow is a concept closely related to everyday life. It may also become an index for leading a better life because it can add pleasure to everyday life.

For example, consider a 9-to-5 office worker. Most such workers consider their jobs as a means of earning money and dedicate most of their lives to unsatisfying work to support their families. They may also work to improve their positions, obtain power, and improve their status. Such extrinsically motivated activity is generally associated with negative mental conditions. Thus, a person engaged daily in an extrinsically motivated activity has a reduced chance of experiencing enjoyment.

In contrast, the implications of the work may be different for other 9-to-5 workers: a certain office worker feels pleasure and joy in the work itself rather than in the material reward to be provided from the work. Such a worker will become absorbed in work for long periods of time. The concept of office hours does not matter for such a worker anymore—the pleasure is in the work itself. This is the state called flow. Neighboring coworkers, superiors, and subordinates may judge this office worker as merely hard working. He or she would not object to this evaluation because he or she does not think about the effort. For example, some elementary school students were playing a PlayStation game for fun overnight. The parent would not tell these children, "do your best to be great." Instead, the children played all night because it was fun—it was not about effort. This also holds true for the office worker described above.

Flow, however, is not just about work. Consider here another example, that of an obese man who begins running to lose weight and become more attractive. In short, he began running out of extrinsic motivation. Running is initially painful for him, and his short distances of running are hardly faster than his walking speed. He sticks with it and gradually his endurance increases, as does his speed Moreover, the pain he experiences from running decreases.

This is a result of his skill level increasing over his challenge level. At first, because his challenge level was high and skill level was low, the man felt uncomfortable and would halt this activity if painful. However, gradually, he comes to see running as fun in itself, and he anticipates it. But now, instead of running to lose weight, he runs for fun. Thus, even the same activity can shift from being extrinsically to intrinsically motivated. The fact that extrinsic motivation can change into intrinsic motivation suggests that the flow could potentially be used for interventions in the health science area.

Measurement of the Flow Experience

A method for measuring flow is essential for a study on flow. In conventional flow studies, the experience sampling method (ESM) has been widely used. A characteristic of ESM is measuring the flow experience as it happens. In the ESM, researchers randomly choose target times from the study time and notify the participant by pager [4, 5]. The participants then answer a questionnaire and report their psychological state as soon as the alarm sounds [4, 5]. An advantage of the ESM is that it is little influenced by recollection bias because a record is created immediately. However, the ESM imposes a large burden on participants a questionnaire method, on the other hand, imposes a smaller burden on the participant and ensures the quantitative objectivity necessary for seriously studying an abstract concept. I will introduce the flow measurement questionnaire below.

The Flow Experience Checklist [6]

The Flow Experience Checklist measured the extent to which the characteristics and the frequency of flow are experienced in everyday life. It contains one item on the frequency of flow experience in daily life. The participant was asked to respond to the questionnaire items on a scale of 1 to 7 (1 = very strongly disagree to 7 = very strongly agree). When answering the questions, participants were asked to observe the following instructions: “Please think of the things you consider fun and fully immersive among your favorite activities. Please recall as much as possible your thoughts and feelings when that activity is going well." The following questions were answered on a scale of 1 to 7: "In day-to-day life, how much of such experience do you have? Please check all those that apply." This score reflects the frequency of the flow experience in daily life.

There were 10 items on the characteristics of the flow experience. These were also scored on a scale of 1 to 7(1 = very strongly disagree to 7 = very strongly agree). There were also 6 items (2 on challenges to goals and 4 on confidence in skills) related to the balance between challenges and skills, which formed a group of variables related to flow conditions, and 4 items on positive emotions and total involvement. This checklist can be used to reduce the burden on the study participants as the number of items is small. Furthermore, this checklist can be converted to various activities; it can be iteratively measured.

Flow Questionnaire [7]

This section measured the degree of the flow experience at the time of a particular activity. The psychological state during participation in activities was measured by 22 items, also scored on a 7-point scale. This scale had six subscales (emotional aspect, satisfaction, activity, concentration, loss of self-consciousness, and sociability), and the following questions were scored on a scale of 1 to 7: "How did you feel during this activity? Please mark ○ for all those that apply." A higher score indicates a deeper flow state.

Flow begins as a psychological issue, and has subsequently been studied for its impacts on sociology, business administration, physical education, pedagogy, and health science. However, work on flow has still been insufficient in the health science area.

In the next chapter, I consider the flow in health science on the basis of empirical research.

References

[1] Csikszentmihalyi M. 1975. *Beyond boredom and anxiety*. San Francisco: Jossey-Bass.

[2] Csikszentmihalyi M. 1990. *Flow: The psychology of optimal experience*. New York: Harper and Row.

[3] Nakamura J, Csikszentmihalyi M. 2002. The concept of flow, *Handbook of Positive Psychology*. New York: Oxford University Press.

[4] Csikszentmihalyi M & Larson, R. 1987 Validity and reliability of the Experience-Sampling Method. *The Journal of Nervous and Mental Disease,* 175, 526–536.

[5] Csikszentmihalyi M, Larson R, & Prescott S. 1977. The ecology of adolescent activity and experience. Journal of Youth and Adolescence, 6, 281–294.

[6] Ishimura I. 2009. Psychological study on enhancing factors and positive functions of flow experiences. Ibaraki: Doctoral thesis from the School of Comprehensive Human Sciences, University of Tsukuba.

[7] Kobayashi R, Takahashi K, Nagatani R, Nagao S, Higashi T, Shirahama K, Sato D, Suzuki M. 2005. Study of validity of flow questionnaire using brain wave. *Jpn J Occup Ther Ment Cognitive Disord* 2005, 2: 70–75.

Chapter 2

The Flow Experience and Brain Activity

Abstract

This chapter will introduce brain activity during flow. I first explain the important function of the prefrontal cortex (PFC) in the brain and present a hypothesis on the relationship between the PFC and the flow experience. Next, I explain near-infrared spectroscopy (NIRS), a method of measuring brain activity. Finally, I describe the activation of the PFC in the brain during flow, and describes its implications for clinical practice.

Flow and the Prefrontal Cortex

In order to better understand the flow, it is necessary to understand brain activity during flow experiences. The PFC is known to be responsible for most higher-order cognitive functions. For example, the PFC is responsible for thinking and creativity, motivation for going live, and memory based on emotion; it is also responsible for executive function. The PFC is to the regions of the cerebral cortex that are anterior to premotor cortex and the supplementary motor area [1]. The PFC occupies approximately a quarter to a third of the human cortex [2].

Previous studies have proposed the transient hypofrontality hypothesis [3,4], which posits that the energy consumption of the PFC is automatically suppressed during the flow experience because energy sources available to the brain are limited [5].

Measurement of Brain Activity

Methods of brain function measurement include functional magnetic resonance imaging (fMRI) and positron emission tomography (PET). There has also been increasing interest in near-infrared spectroscopy (NIRS) as a method of measuring brain function in addition to fMRI and PET. This is because it is noninvasive and allows measurements to be taken in a natural environment without physically constraining the participant, unlike fMRI and PET. It is both easy on subjects and easily allows repeated measurements. Furthermore, NIRS measuring devices are small and inexpensive, and resolution is relatively high. Therefore, NIRS can be used with a wide range of subjects (such as those with schizophrenia [6], major depressive disorders [7], traumatic brain injuries [8], bipolar disorder [9], pediatric attention-deficit/hyperactivity disorder [10], coronary artery disease [11], multiple sclerosis [12], post-traumatic stress disorder [13], eating disorders [14], obsessive-compulsive disorder [15], and Alzheimer's disease [16]).

NIRS is capable of measuring hemoglobin oxygen metabolic changes in vivo using near-infrared light with high bio-permeability [17]. NIRS calculates the hemoglobin concentration change based on the hemoglobin absorption spectrum and the modified Beer–Lambert law [17]. The validity of NIRS has been confirmed from the relationship between fMRI [18].

Cognitive Tasks Used in the NIRS Study

NIRS was used to measure brain activity of participants in this chapter during cognitive tasks. Various cognitive tasks were used in the NIRS study (e.g., a verbal fluency task [19], [20]; Stroop task [21]; Wisconsin card sorting test [22]; and the Uchida–Kraepelin psycho-diagnostic test [23]). The verbal fluency task (VFT) in particular is a frequently used cognitive task because it does not need special equipment and can be carried out in a relatively short time. In the VFT, "a," "i," "u," "e," and "o" in Japanese are simply repeated as a baseline task, then, as the target task, participants generate as many words starting with an assigned sound as possible. Not only does this require recall of words from long-term memory, it also requires complex recognition functions such as working memory, remembering the words previously answered, restraint against using inappropriate words, and sustained concentration [24].

Activation of the PFC in the Brain during a Flow Experience Using NIRS

Study participants were healthy college students comprising 60 people (mean age: 19.52 ± 0.96 years: 38 males and 22 females). All participants were right handed. Here, a 2-channel NIRS machine (PocketNIRS; DynaSense Inc., Japan), operated at 735 nm, 810 nm, and 850 nm in the infrared light spectrum, was used to measure relative changes in the concentrations of oxygenated hemoglobin ([oxy-Hb]) and deoxygenated hemoglobin ([deoxy-Hb]). Adhesive sheets were used to place two probes on the foreheads of participants and were centered on the Fp1 and Fp2 positions according to the international 10/20 system. I assessed prefrontal activation as the average difference between the pre-task [oxy-Hb] and during-task. The activation task consisted of a 30-s pre-task baseline, a 60-s VFT, and a 30-s post-task baseline performed while the participant was seated in a chair. The participants were instructed to keep their head immobile as much as possible, to keep their eyes open, and to not speak. A block design was used in which a target object baseline was repeated thrice alternately with the challenge task. For the pre- and post-task baseline periods, the participants were instructed to repeat Japanese vowels (/a/, /i/, /u/, /e/, and /o/) slowly during the period. These repetitions were intended to correct the fluency task data for activation because of vocalization. During VFT, the participants were instructed to generate as many Japanese words beginning with a designated syllable as possible. In this study, 3 initial syllables (1: /a/, /o/, /to/; 2: /ha/, /ka/, /se/; 3: /ta/, /i/, /ki/) were presented to the participants in a counterbalanced order, and each syllable was changed every 20s during the 60-s task. During VFT, the participants changed syllables every 20s to reduce the time during which they remained silent or gave up the task.

I examined the relationship between the degree of the flow state and prefrontal activity during VFT [20]. Correlation analysis was used to describe the strength and direction of the relationship between the variables. Pearson correlations were used. The flow questionnaire (FQ) was used to measure the extent of the flow state during the VFT [25]. PFC activity during the VFT was measured using a two-channel NIRS. Scores on the flow questionnaire during the VFT are shown in Figure 1. The average of the subscales in the FQ are Emotional aspect (4.2 ± 0.7), Satisfaction (3.8 ± 0.8), Activity (4.4 ± 0.8), Concentration (5.2 ± 0.9), Loss of self-consciousness (4 ± 0.9), and Sociability (4 ± 0.9). The mean baseline of left PFC and right PFC were 0.0197 ± 0.0502 (au) and 0.0255 ± 0.0452 (au), respectively. The mean during the task of left PFC and right PFC were 0.0324 ± 0.0578 (au) and 0.0372 ± 0.0537 (au), respectively.

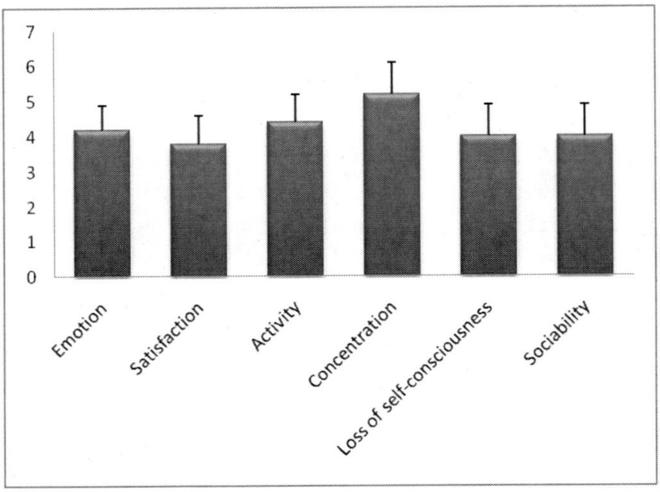

Figure 1. Scores on the flow questionnaire during the verbal fluency task.

The mean left PFC and right PFC changes in [oxy-Hb] were 0.013 ± 0.018 (au) and 0.012 ± 0.018 (au), respectively. The average number of generated words in VFT was 14.7 ± 3.9. Task performance was significantly correlated with the 5 FQ subcategories (Emotional aspect, Satisfaction, Activity, Concentration, and Sociability). Correlations between satisfaction scores in the FQ and oxy-Hb changes in the PFC are shown in Figures 2 and 3. Oxy-Hb changes during the task were significantly negatively correlated with the satisfaction scores on the FQ in the left and right PFC. In brief, I show that prefrontal activity is low when there is high satisfaction in the flow state at task time. This result supports the transient hypofrontality hypothesis [5]).

In clinical practice, there is a scene that provides flow activities for the patient. At that time, it is necessary for the therapist to know if the patient's PFC is in a low activity state. Therapists should avoid assigning flow activities to patients in order to raise their PFC activity.

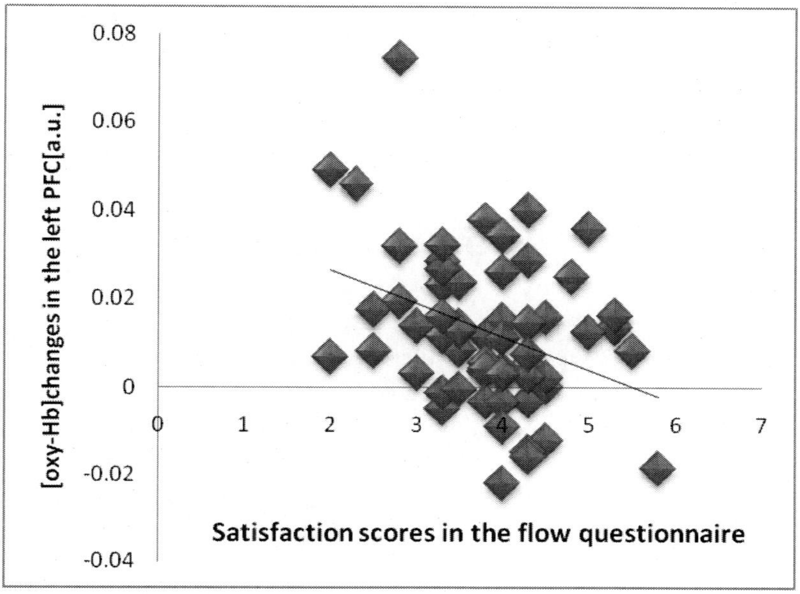

Figure 2. Correlations between satisfaction scores in the flow questionnaire and oxy-Hb changes in the left prefrontal cortex.

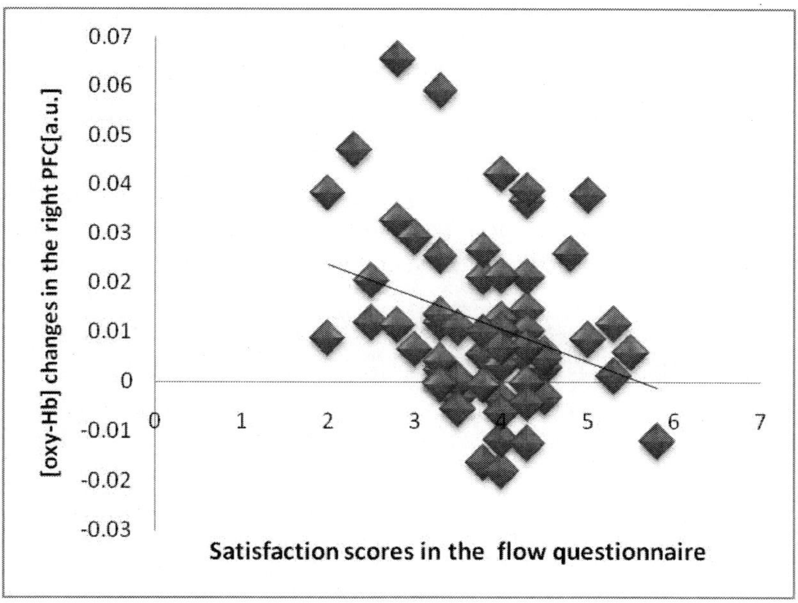

Figure 3. Correlations between satisfaction scores in the flow questionnaire and oxy-Hb changes in the right prefrontal cortex.

This chapter is based on Hirao K. 2014. Prefrontal hemodynamic responses and the degree of flow experience among occupational therapy students during their performance of a cognitive task. *J Educ Eval Health Prof.* 11:24.

References

[1] Zelazo PD & Muller U. 2002. Executive functions in typical and atypical development. In U. Goswami (Ed.), *Handbook of childhood cognitive development*. Oxford, UK: Blackwell.

[2] Fuster JM. 2008. *The prefrontal cortex*, 4th edn. London, UK: Elsevier.

[3] Dietrich A. 2003. Functional neuroanatomy of altered states of consciousness: The transient hypofrontality hypothesis. *Conscious Cogn.* 12(2), 231–256.

[4] Dietrich A. 2006. Transient hypofrontality as a mechanism for the psychological effects of exercise. *Psychiatry Res.* 145, 79–83.

[5] Dietrich A. 2004. Neurocognitive mechanisms underlying the experience of flow. *Conscious Cogn.* 13, 746–761.

[6] Quan W, Wu T, Li Z, Wang Y, Dong W, Lv B. 2014. Reduced prefrontal activation duringa verbal fluency task in Chinese-speaking patients with schizophrenia as measured by near-infrared spectroscopy. *Prog Neuropsychopharmacol Biol Psychiatry*, Dec 24;58C:51–58.

[7] Akashi H, Tsujii N, Mikawa W, Adachi T, Kirime E, Shirakawa O. 2014. Prefrontal cortex activation is associated with a discrepancy between self- and observer-rated depression severities of major depressive disorder: A multichannel near-infrared spectroscopy study. *J Affect Disord.*174C:165–172.

[8] Vilkė A, Bilskienė D, Šaferis V, Gedminas M, Bieliauskaitė D, Tamašauskas A, Macas A. 2014. Predictive value of early near-infrared spectroscopy monitoring of patients with traumatic brain injury. *Medicina (Kaunas)* 50(5):263–8.

[9] Mikawa W, Tsujii N, Akashi H, Adachi T, Kirime E, Shirakawa O. 2015 Left temporal activation associated with depression severity during a verbal fluency task in patients with bipolar disorder: A multichannel near-infrared spectroscopy study. *J Affect Disord.* 173:193–200.

[10] Ota T, Iida J, Nakanishi Y, Sawada S, Matsuura H, Yamamuro K, Ueda S, Uratani M, Kishimoto N, Negoro H, Kishimoto T. 2014. Increased

prefrontal hemodynamic change after atomoxetine administration in pediatric attention-deficit/hyperactivity disorder as measured by near-infrared spectroscopy. *Psychiatry Clin Neurosci.*2014 Oct 30. doi: 10.1111/pcn.12251.

[11] Dohi T, Maehara A, Moreno PR, Baber U, Kovacic JC, Limaye AM, Ali ZA, Sweeny JM, Mehran R, Dangas GD, Xu K, Sharma SK, Mintz GS, Kini AS. 2015. The relationship among extent of lipid-rich plaque, lesion characteristics, and plaque progression/regression in patients with coronary artery disease: A serial near-infrared spectroscopy and intravascular ultrasound study. *Eur Heart J Cardiovasc Imaging.* 2015 Jan;16(1):81–7.

[12] Jimenez JJ, Yang R, Nathoo N, Varshney VP, Golestani AM, Goodyear BG, Metz LM, Dunn JF. 2014. Detection of reduced interhemispheric cortical communication during task execution in multiple sclerosis patients using functional near-infrared spectroscopy. *J Biomed Opt.* Jul;19(7):076008.

[13] Tian F, Yennu A, Smith-Osborne A, Gonzalez-Lima F, North CS, Liu H. 2014 Prefrontal responses to digit span memory phases in patients with post-traumatic stress disorder (PTSD): A functional near infrared spectroscopy study. *Neuroimage Clin.* 13;4:808–19.

[14] Katayama H, Kohmura K, Tanaka S, Imaeda M, Kawano N, Noda Y, Nishioka K, Ando M, Aleksic B, Iidaka T, Ozaki N.2014 Social insecurity in relation to orbitofrontal activity in patients with eating disorders: A near-infrared spectroscopy study. *BMC Psychiatry.* Jun 12;14:173.

[15] Nakanishi M, Oshita H, Tanaka Y, Inoue A, Kawashima C, Okamoto K, Kobayashi S, Ishitobi Y, Ninomiya T, Akiyoshi J.2014. Near-infrared spectroscopy during the Verbal Fluency Task before and after treatment with image exposure and SSRI Therapy in patients with obsessive-compulsive disorder. *Case Rep Psychiatry.*2014:591023.

[16] Kito H, Ryokawa A, Kinoshita Y, Sasayama D, Sugiyama N, Ogihara T, Yasaki T, Hagiwara T, Inuzuka S, Takahashi T, Genno H, Nose H, Hanihara T, Washizuka S, Amano N. 2014. Comparison of alterations in cerebral hemoglobin oxygenation in late life depression and Alzheimer's disease as assessed by near-infrared spectroscopy. *Behav Brain Funct.* 17;10:8.

[17] Sakatani K. 2012. *NIRS: Basic and clinical applications.* Shinkoh Igaku Shuppan Co., LTD Tokyo.

[18] Strangman G, Culver JP, Thompson JH, Boas DA. A. 2002. Quantitative comparison of simultaneous BOLD fMRI and NIRS recordings during functional brain activation. *Neuroimage* 17:719–731.

[19] Hirao K.2014 Two-channel Near-infrared Spectroscopic analysis of association of paranoia symptoms with prefrontal activation. *Clin Psychopharmacol Neurosci.* 12(3):218–21.

[20] Hirao K. 2014. Prefrontal hemodynamic responses and the degree of flow experience among occupational therapy students during their performance of a cognitive task. *J Educ Eval Health Prof.* 2014 Sep 30;11:24.

[21] Zhang L, Sun J, Sun B, Luo Q, Gong H. 2014. Studying hemispheric lateralization during a Stroop task through near-infrared spectroscopy-based connectivity. *J Biomed Opt.* 2014 May;19(5):57012.

[22] Hashimoto K, Uruma G, Abo M. 2008. Activation of the prefrontal cortex during the Wisconsin card sorting test (Keio Version) as measured by two-channel near-infrared spectroscopy in patients with traumatic brain injury. Eur Neurol. 59(1-2):24–30.

[23] Higashi T, Sone Y, Ogawa K, Kitamura YT, Saiki K, Sagawa S, Yanagida T, Seiyama A. 2004. Changes in regional cerebral blood volume in the frontal cortex during mental work with and without caffeine intake: Functional monitoring using near-infrared spectroscopy. *J Biomed Opt.* Jul-Aug; 9(4):788–93.

[24] Henry JD, Crawford JR.2004. A meta-analytic review of verbal fluency performance following focal cortical lesions. *Neuropsychology.* 18: 284–295.

[25] Kobayashi R, Takahashi K, Nagatani R, Nagao S, Higashi T, Shirahama K, Sato D, Suzuki M. 2005. Study of validity of flow questionnaire using brain waves. *Jpn J Occup Ther Ment Cognitive Disord* 2: 70–75.

Chapter 3

The Flow Experience and Subjective and Objective Stress

Abstract

This chapter introduces the influence of the flow experience on subjective and objective stress. First, I present a summary of stress. Next, I introduce a method of measuring subjective and objective stress; then I argue that high flow is helpful for reducing subjective stress.

Finally, I note that high flow does not contribute to reducing objective stress.

Stress

Stress is a human reaction to an external stimulus [1]. One cannot avoid stress during life. Moderate stress can be beneficial, but excessive stress can harm one's quality of life; for example, stress is positively associated with suicidal ideation [2]. Thus, it is important to reduce stress in modern society.

To do so, it is necessary to first measure stress. This chapter used the visual analogue scale (VAS), an index of subjective stress [3]. Respondents specified their levels of subjective stress by drawing a straight line at a right angle through a 10-cm line between two points, which indicated "no stress" on the left and "maximum stress" on the right. The distance along the line was measured from the left end of the VAS to measure stress.

Biomarkers can serve as indicators of objective stress. Biomarkers are indices that provide information from the living body in the form of the density of chemical substances from body samples such as blood, stroma liquid, saliva, and urine. When a person is exposed to mental stress, two kinds of physical stress reactions are known to be activated [4]. One is a hypothalamus-pituitary-adrenal (HPA) reaction, the other a sympatho-adrenal medullar (SAM) reaction. Activation of the SAM system increases the secretion of salivary amylase [5, 6]. Some research has suggested that it may be possible to measure discomfort and comfort by salivary amylase activity (AMY) [7]. In recent years of stress research, salivary AMY has been used as a biochemical indicator of stress because it is known to measure sympathetic activity [6]. A salivary AMY monitor (Nipro Co., Japan) and test strips (Nipro Co., Japan) have been used to measure objective stress [8, 9]. In brief, a test strip was inserted under the subject's tongue for 30 seconds, then the monitor took approximately 1 min to return results.

We examined the degree of flow subjects experienced while listening to music and its effect on subjective and objective stress [3]. One week prior to the study, the participants listened to six pieces of classical or healing music and selected the two pieces that they found the most inoffensive. It took approximately 10 minutes to listen to each two pieces of music. We enrolled 103 healthy college students who provided written consent after being given a verbal explanation of the study. Four students had missing questionnaire responses and were excluded from analysis. The remaining 99 participants included in this analysis (44 men and 55 women) had a mean age of 19.7 ± 0.9 years. Participants were classified into a high score group and a low score group based on the average flow score (96.27±12.11) and each average subscale score: emotion (4.49±0.62), satisfaction (4.22±0.79), activity (4.27±0.61), concentration (3.74±0.79), loss of self-consciousness (4.85±0.92), and sociability (4.57±0.80).

Pre-intervention and post-intervention VAS and AMY values, and the percent change of each value, were compared between the high score group and the low score group for the flow scale and each of the subscales using the Mann-Whitney test.

The percent (%) change was calculated as (postvalue - prevalue)/ prevalue ×100.

Specifically, we compared the rate of change (using VAS and AMY) before and after listening to music in high and low flow groups.

The Flow Experience and Subjective Stress

There was no significant difference in the pre-intervention VAS value between the high score group (42.36 ± 21.06) and the low score group (46.04 ± 21.69) (p = 0.46). Similarly, there were no significant differences in the subscale scores before intervention. However, there was a significant difference in the post-intervention VAS value between the high score group (28.19 ±17.39) and the low score group (38.56±23.07) (p = 0.03). Among the subscales, emotion (p = 0.04), satisfaction (p=0.03), and loss of self-consciousness (p = 0.003) showed significant differences between the groups after intervention.

Figure 1 shows a comparison of subjective stress (VAS values) between the high flow and low flow groups. The percentage change in flow score was significantly different in the high and low flow groups, showing that experiencing high flow can help reduce subjective stress. I describe the result of the comparison in the lower item of the flow in the following discussion.

Figure 2 shows a comparison of subjective stress (VAS values) between the high emotion and low emotion groups. The percentage change in the emotion score was significantly different in the high emotion and low emotion groups, showing that high emotion is helpful for reducing subjective stress. This result suggests that positive emotions such as pleasure, joy, delight, and pride help decrease stress.

Figure 3 compares the subjective stress (VAS values) of the high and low satisfaction groups. The percentage change in the satisfaction score differed significantly between the high and low satisfaction groups. In other words, high satisfaction can help reduce subjective stress. This suggests that stress decreases with the presence of sensations of accomplishment, completeness, and getting one's way. Figure 4 shows a comparison of subjective stress (VAS values) between the high activity and low activity groups. The percentage change in the activity score differed significantly in the high activity and the low activity groups, showing that a high level of activity is helpful for reducing subjective stress. These results suggest that being strong, aggressive, and animated helps reduce stress.

Figure 5 shows a comparison of subjective stress (VAS values) between high of self-consciousness and low loss of self-consciousness groups. The percentage change in loss of self-consciousness score differed significantly in the high and the low loss groups, showing that a high loss of self-consciousness is helpful for reducing subjective stress. This result suggests that experiencing relaxation, freedom, and openness are helpful in reducing stress.

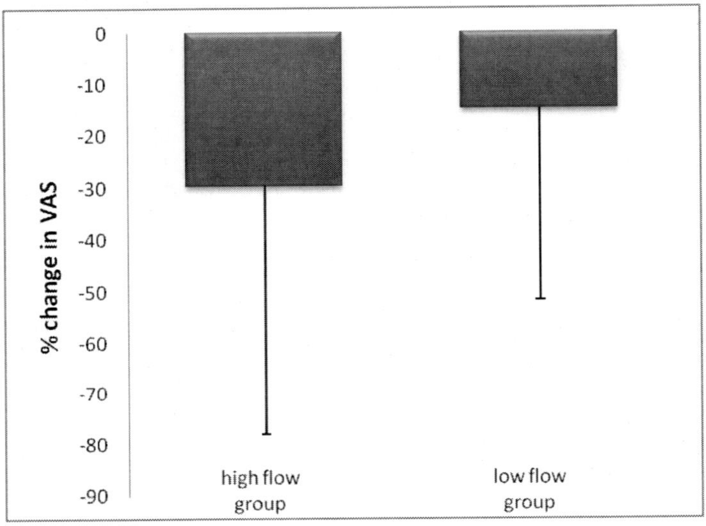

Figure 1. Comparison of subjective stress (VAS) between the high flow and low flow groups.

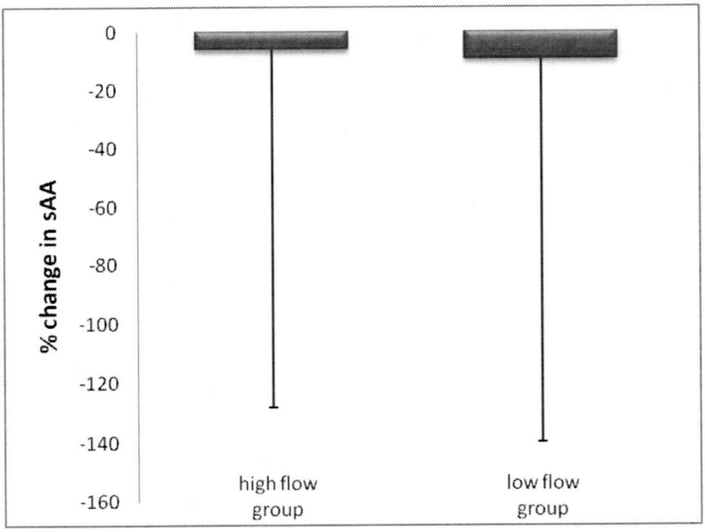

Figure 2. Comparison of subjective stress (VAS) between the high and low emotion groups.

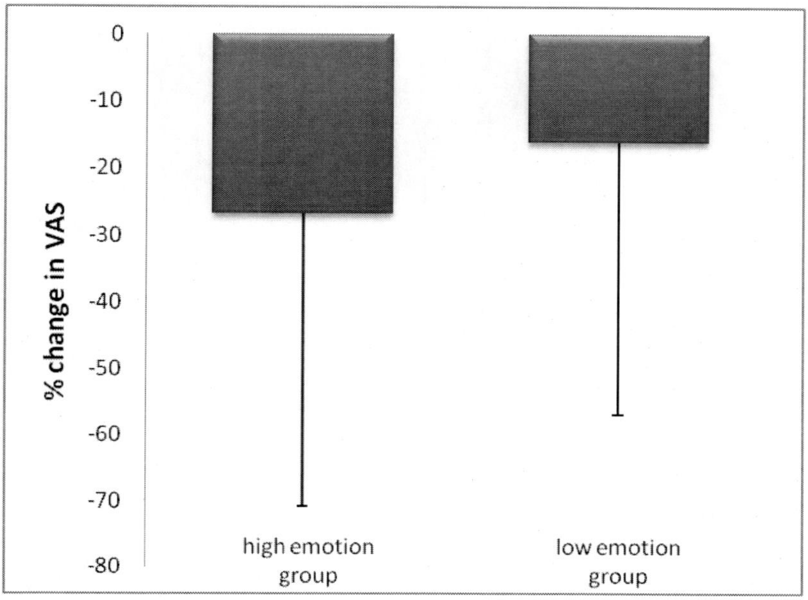

Figure 3. Comparison of subjective stress (VAS) between the high and low satisfaction groups.

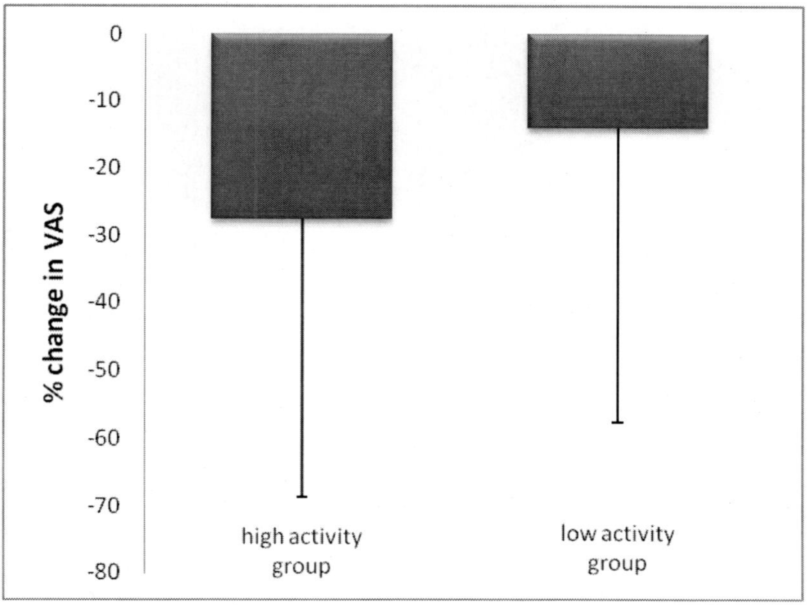

Figure 4. Comparison of subjective stress (VAS) between the high and low activity groups.

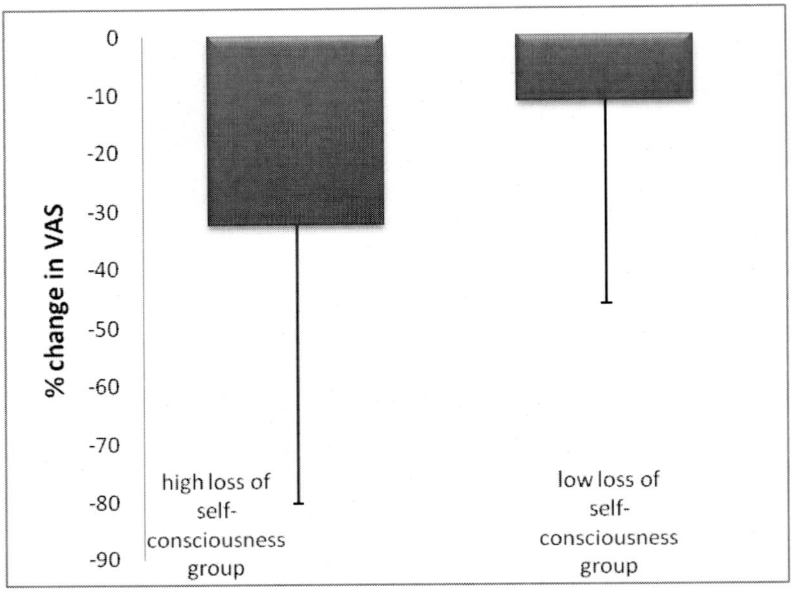

Figure 5. Comparison of subjective stress (VAS) between the high and low loss of self-consciousness groups.

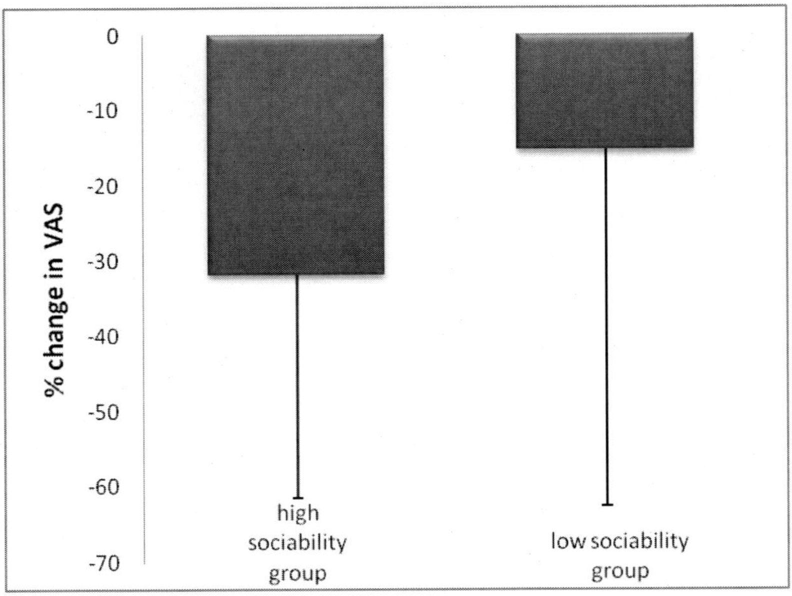

Figure 6. Comparison of subjective stress (VAS) between the high and the low sociability groups.

Figure 6 compares the subjective stress (VAS values) of the high and low sociability groups. The percentage change in sociability score differed significantly in the high and low sociability groups, showing that high sociability is helpful for reducing subjective stress. This suggests that feelings of friendship and togetherness can help reduce stress.

Flow Experience and Objective Stress

There was no significant difference in pre-intervention AMY values between the high score group (86.67 ± 82.17 kU/l) and the low score group (64.27 ± 54.89 kU/l) ($p = 0.54$). There were also no significant differences in the subscales before intervention. In addition, no significant difference in post-intervention AMY values was noted between the high score group (30.21 ± 27.93 kU/l) and the low score group (34.32 ± 33.86 kU/l) ($p = 0.32$), while no significant differences in the subscales were found after intervention.

Figure 2 compares indicators of objective stress (salivary AMY values) between the high stress and low stress groups. The percentage change in flow score did not show any significant difference between the high score and low score groups. This demonstrates that high flow does not contribute to reducing objective stress. The reason for this is unclear. A potential reason is that the standard deviation value of salivary AMY is large. Therefore, there is a need to consider using a blood-derived stress marker in future research.

This chapter is based on a study first reported in Hirao K, Kobayashi R, Okishima K, Tomokuni Y, Yabuwaki K. Influence of different intensities of brief flow experiences on subjective and objective stress. *Med Biol* 155(10): 713–720. 2011.

References

[1] Selye H. 1978. *The Stress of Life*. McGraw-Hill,.

[2] Shang L, Li J, Li Y, Wang T, Siegrist J. 2014. Stressful psychosocial school environment and suicidal ideation in Chinese adolescents. *Soc Psychiatry Psychiatr Epidemiol*. 49(2):205–10.

[3] Hirao K, Kobayashi R, Okishima K, Tomokuni Y, Yabuwaki K.2011. Influence of different intensities of brief flow experiences on subjective and objective stress. *Med Biol* 155(10): 713–720.

[4] Maier SF, Watkins LR. 1998. Cytokines for psychologists: implications of bidirectional immune-to-brain communication for understanding behavior, mood, and cognition. *Psychol Rev.* 105(1):83–107.

[5] Groza P, et al. 1971. Postoperative salivary amylase changes in children. *Rev Roum Physiol.*;8:307–312.

[6] Speirs RL, Herring J, Cooper WD, Hardy CC, Hind CRK:1974. The influence of sympathetic activity and isoprenaline on the secretion of amylase from the human parotid gland. *Archs Oral Biol* 19: 747–752.

[7] Takai N, et al. Effect of psychological stress on the salivary cortisol and amylase levels in healthy young adults. *Arch Oral Biol.* 2004;49:963–968.

[8] Yamaguchi M, Kanemaru M, Kanemori T, Mizuno Y:2003 Flow-injection-type biosensor system for salivary amylase activity. Biosens Bioelectron 18: 835–840.

[9] Yamaguchi M, Kanemori T, Kanemaru M, Takai N, Mizuno Y, Yoshida H. 2004. Performance evaluation of salivary amylase activity monitor. *Biosens Bioelectron* 20: 491–497.

Chapter 4

The Flow Experience and Quality of Life

Abstract

This chapter introduces the relationship between flow and quality of life (QOL). I first present an overview of QOL. Next, I introduce method for measuring health-related QOL, defining it as the relationship among flow experiences in younger and older adults.

Quality of Life

The WHO defined QOL as an individual's perceptions in the context of their culture and value systems, in relation to their personal goals, standards, and concerns [1]. QOL is an important indicator in the health science area. The Medical Outcome Study 36-Item Short-Form Health Survey (SF-36) in particular has been widely used [2–4]. The SF-8, a shortened version of the SF-36, has also been widely used [5]. The SF-8 and SF-36 address so-called health-related QOL, which can potentially be improved or worsened by particular medical interventions addressing QOL measurements [5]. A national standard level of 50 has been established for SF-8[5].

The following eight subscales and two-component summary of SF-8 were used in this chapter: physical functioning (PF), which reflects the ability to carry out activities [5]; role-physical (RP), which reflects the presence or absence of physical problems during work and normal activities [5]; bodily pain (BP), which reflects the degree to which usual work is impeded by pain [5]; general health (GH), which reflects overall quality of health [5]; vitality (VT), which reflects perceptions of one's own vitality [5]; social functioning (SF), which reflects the degree to which physical or psychological issues hinder relationships[5]; role-emotional (RE), which reflects the presence or absence of psychological problems in work and normal activities [5]; and mental health (MH), which reflects overall mood [5]. Two summary scores, the physical component summary (PCS) and mental component summary (MCS), are calculated from these eight subscales [5].

Flow Experience and Quality of Life among Young Adults

Here, I introduce the relationship between flow and HRQOL, first focusing on young adults [6]. Study participants were 50 healthy college students (8 men and 42 women). The average age of the subjects was 18.46 years (SD = 0.54). In this chapter, flow experiences were assessed with the Flow Experience Checklist [7], and HRQOL was assessed with the SF-8 [5]. For statistical processing, Spearman's rank correlation coefficient analysis was used to assess the correlations between the scores for the Flow Experience Checklist and the SF-8. The frequency of flow experiences was 4.25±1.69, the time spent on important daily activities was 7.99±8.41 hours per week, and the total flow score was 51.16±8.6, while the score for challenge to goals was 10±3.25, that for confidence in skills was 18.64±4.01, and that for positive emotions and awareness was 22.52 ± 3.6. The most important activities of daily living among the participants are shown in Figure 1 (more than half of the participants had cited sports). The most important activity in daily life was sport (n = 27, 54%), relaxation and entertainment (n = 12, 24%), social activity (n = 1, 2%), art and music (n = 6, 12%), or others (n = 4, 8%).I measured the degree of flow for these activities. The average scores on the SF-8 are shown in Figure 2. The SF-8 scores were 49.33±5.31 for physical functioning 49.58±5.16 for physical role, 51.73±8.61 for bodily pain 49.56 ±7.42 for general health perception, 49.92±7.03 for vitality, 46.64±8.09 for social functioning, 47.1±6.41 for emotional role, 43.94±7.36 for mental health, 51.17±5.03 for PCS, and 43.59±6.63 for MCS. The PCS exceeded the nation standard, but the MCS was below this standard. Participants were evaluated as having low mental QOL scores.

The frequency of flow experiences showed a significant positive correlation with the timing of the activity. Flow occurred frequently when activity times were long. The frequency of flow experiences showed a significant positive correlation with GH. This suggests that good health promotes a high frequency of flow in everyday life. The frequency of flow experiences showed a significant positive correlation with SF, suggesting that positive experiences in relationships promote a high frequency of flow in everyday life. At first glance, flow appears to be egocentric because it involves becoming fully absorbed in something. However, the flow experience in reality is not egocentric at all and can be associated with another person. The frequency of flow also has a significant positive correlation with the MCS. It is possible that given its positive effect on mental QOL, flow should be experienced frequently in daily life. Therefore, flow should be promoted as part of mental health promotion.

An interesting result is that the total flow score did not correlate significantly with all the SF-8 scores. The total flow score reflected the degree to which flow was experienced. The degree of flow was measured for a single particular activity in daily life. Therefore, when they measure the degree of the flow for plural activity, different results may appear.

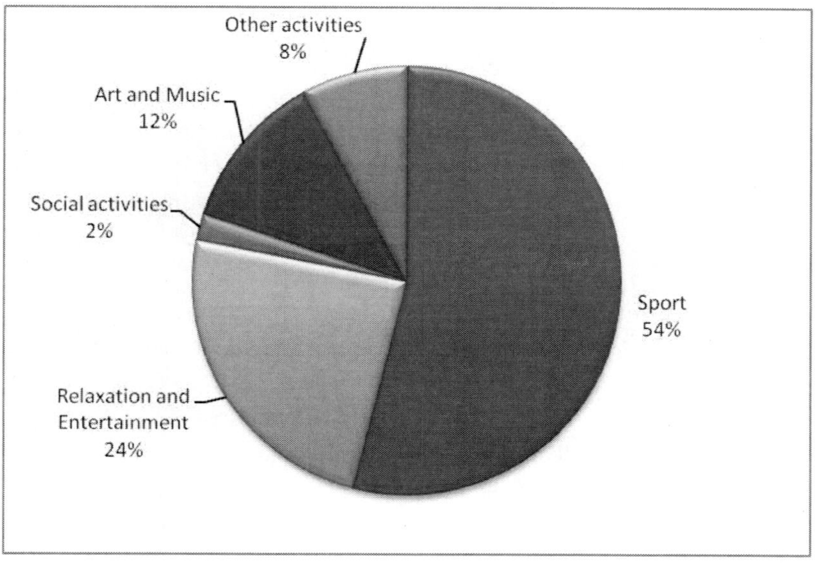

Figure 1. The most important activities of daily living.

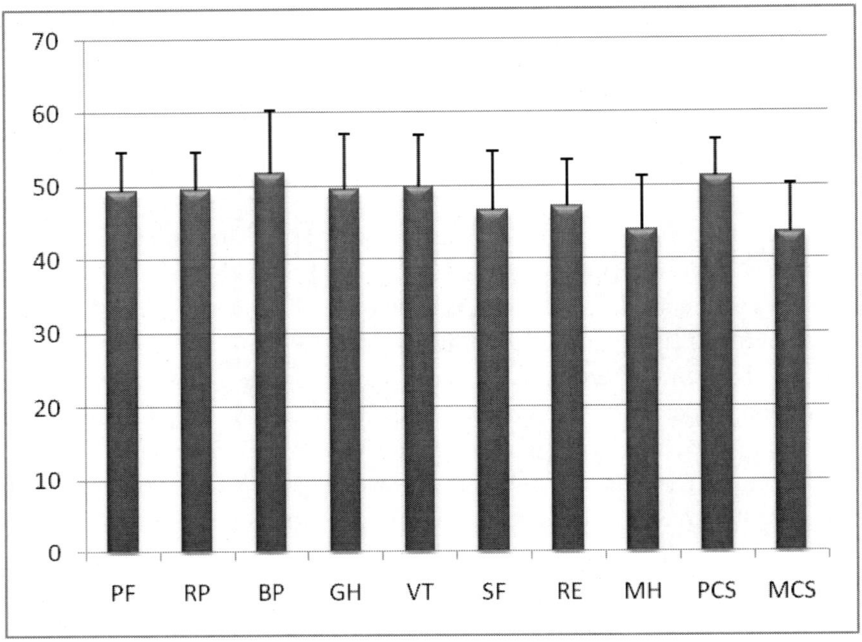

Figure 2. Scores on the Medical Outcome Study 8-Item Short-Form Health Survey (SF-8).

The Flow Experience and Quality of Life among Older Adults

Here, I discuss the relationship between flow and HRQOL among older adults [8]. Study participants were 119 healthy elderly persons (45 men and 74 women) living in rural areas who participated in a "meeting for the elderly" that occurred at a nursing home. Their mean age was 77.7 ± 5.6 years. This chapter classified the following four groups: an apathetic group (n = 35, 29.4%), anxious group (n = 16, 13.4%), relaxed group (n = 25, 21%), and flow group (n = 43, 36.1%). These classifications were determined by challenge level (Mean = 10.12, SD = 2.38) and skill level (Mean = 19.87, SD = 4.15) as determined by the Flow Experience Checklist [7]. Questionnaire forms were distributed in the hall where all participants gathered, and were completed after a detailed explanation of the questionnaire was given by the authors. The questionnaire forms were collected immediately by the authors. This survey was conducted four times by the authors from May 2010 to December 2010 as an adjunct to routine health checks. Each of the four surveys targeted different participants. One-way analysis of variance was performed for four groups (apathetic, anxious, related, and flow) using the dependent variables of age, gender, frequency of flow experience, duration of activity, SF-8 score. Tukey's test was used for multiple comparisons.

The frequency of flow experiences was 5.08 ± 1.4, the time spent on important daily activities was 11.61 ± 10.6 hours per week, and the total flow score was 51.22 ± 9.4, while the score for challenge to goals was 10.12 ± 2.38, that for confidence in skills was 19.87 ± 4.15, and that for positive emotions and awareness was 21.24 ± 4.34.

The SF-8 scores were 45.47 ± 7.63 for physical functioning, 45.77 ± 7.89 for physical role, 46.21 ± 7.83 for bodily pain, 49.31 ± 6.58 for general health perception, 50.53 ± 6.11 for vitality, 46.3 ± 8.19 for social functioning, 47.92 ± 6.69 for emotional role, 49.39 ± 5.92 for mental health, 44.52 ± 7.19 for PCS, and 49.38 ± 6.07 for MCS.

A comparison of the physical functioning scores in the SF-8 for the four groups is shown in Figure 3. PF was significantly different in the relaxed and apathetic groups, showing that those who felt relaxed during important daily activities had better body function than the apathetic group. Therefore, a relaxed state may be beneficial for body function in older adults. The direction of cause and effect, however, remains undetermined. Therefore, it is necessary to interpret these results cautiously.

Figure 4 compares the RP scores of the four groups in the SF-8. RP scores differed significantly between the flow and apathetic groups, the relaxed and apathetic groups, and the anxious and apathetic groups. Therefore, an apathetic state may negatively impact physical function. This state may impede positive actions and movement, even for important activities. Therefore it may negatively impact personal activity.

Figure 5 compares the GH scores of the four groups in the SF-8. The GH scores differed significantly in the flow and apathetic groups. Therefore, older adults in the flow state are possibly in better health than those in the apathetic state. It may also be possible that older adults in good health may experience flow more easily. In either case, flow and health condition have a mutual relationship in older adults.

Figure 6 compares the physical component summary of the SF-8 scores among the four groups. The PCS scores differed significantly between the flow and apathetic groups, and the relaxed and apathetic groups. Physical QOL appears to be higher in the flow (high levels of challenge and skills) and the relaxed (low level of challenge and a high level of skills) groups than the apathetic (low levels of challenge and skills) group.

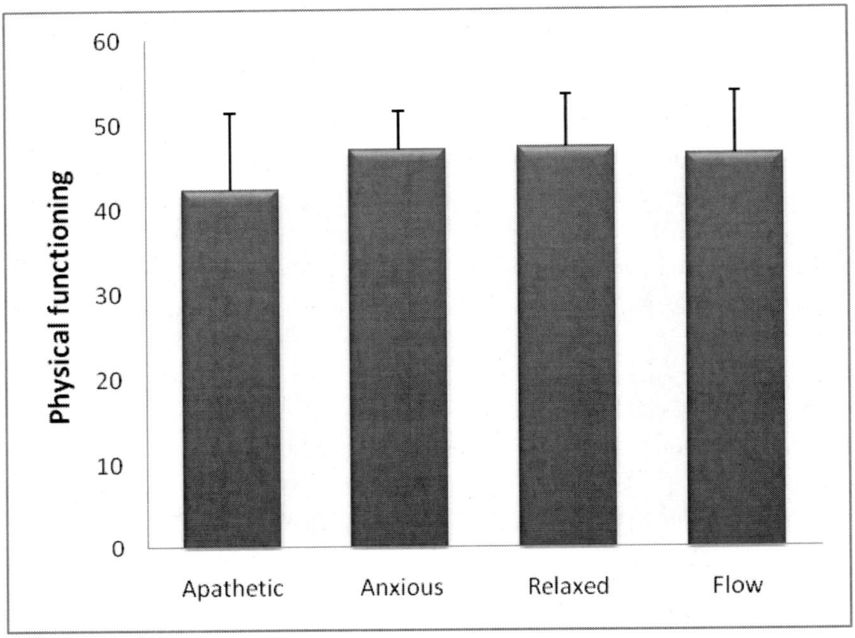

Figure 3. Comparison of physical functioning SF-8 scores of the four groups.

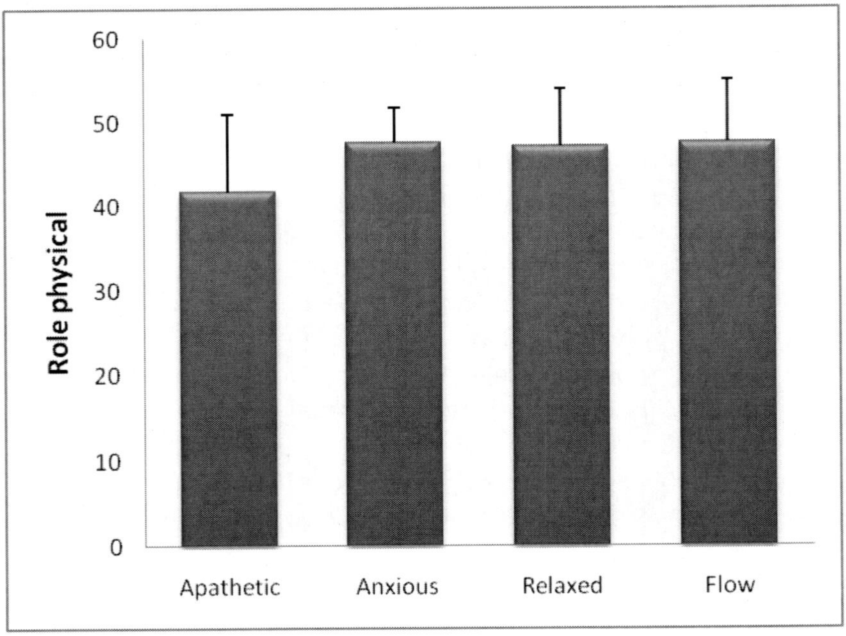

Figure 4. Comparison of the role-physical SF-8 scores of the four groups.

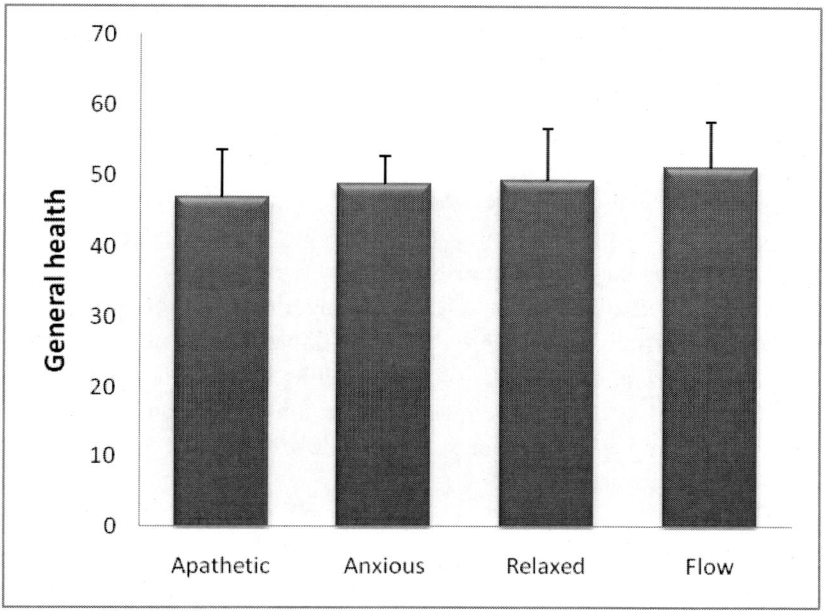

Figure 5. Comparison of the general health SF-8 scores of the four groups.

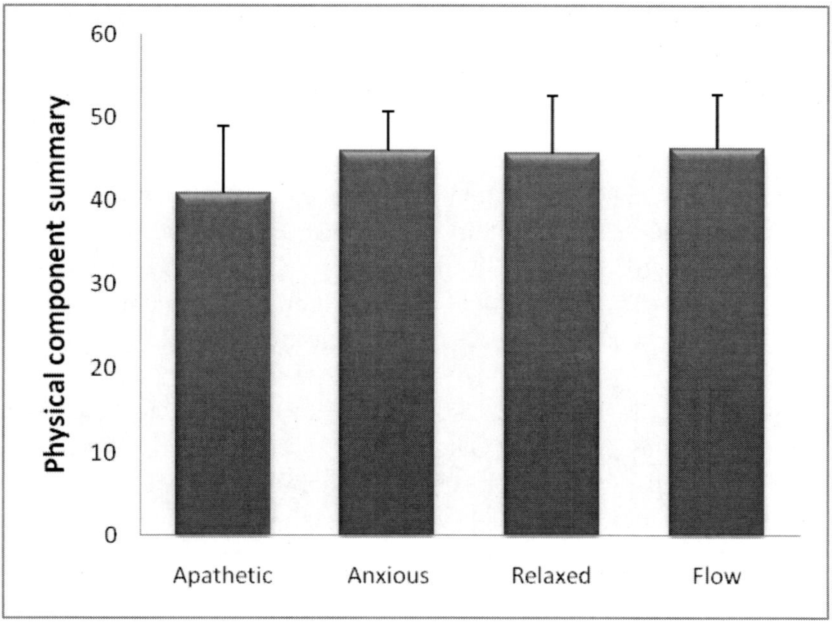

Figure 6. Comparison of the physical component summary of SF-8 scores of the four groups.

The common feature of the flow and relaxed groups is a high challenge level. Here, this refers not to objective ability, but to whether an individual is subjectively recognized as having a high capacity for challenge. Therefore, increasing confidence in one's ability may increase one's physical QOL. In addition, the elderly may not necessarily need a good flow state for QOL. As they approach the end of life, they may prefer a stable everyday life over new challenges.

This chapter is based on Hirao K, Kobayashi R, Okishima K, Tomokuni Y. 2011. Influence of flow experience during daily life on health-related quality of life and salivary amylase activity in Japanese college students. *Jpn. J. Occup. Med. Traumatol* 59: 13–18 and Hirao K, Kobayashi R, Okishima K, Tomokuni Y. 2012. Flow experience and health-related quality of life in community dwelling elderly Japanese. *Nurs Health Sci* 14(1): 52–57.

References

[1] Kuyken, W, Orley, J, Power, M, Herrman, H, Schofield, H, & Murphy, B. 1995. The World Health Organization quality of life assessment (WHOQOL): Position paper from the World Health Organization. *Social Science & Medicine*, 41, 1403–1409.

[2] Fukuhara S.et al. 1998. Translation, adaptation, and validation of the SF-36 Health Survey for use in Japan. *Journal of Clinical Epidemiology*, 51,11:1037–1044.

[3] Fukuhara S.et al: 1998. Psychometric and clinical tests of validity of the Japanese SF-36 Health Survey, *Journal of Clinical Epidemiology*, 51,11:1045–1053.

[4] Ware, JE.et al 1992.The MOS 36-Item Short-Form Health Survey (SF-36).I. Conceptual framework and item selection. *Medical Care*, 30:473–483.

[5] Fukuhara S, Suzukamo Y. 2004 Manual of the SF-8 Japanese version, Kyoto, Institute for Health Outcomes & Process Evaluation Research.

[6] Hirao K, Kobayashi R, Okishima K, Tomokuni Y. 2011. Influence of flow experience during daily life on health-related quality of life and salivary amylase activity in Japanese college students. *Jpn. J. Occup. Med. Traumatol* 59: 13–18.

[7] Ishimura I. 2009. Psychological study on enhancing factors and positive functions of flow experiences. Ibaraki: Doctoral thesis from the School of Comprehensive Human Sciences, University of Tsukuba.

[8] Hirao K, Kobayashi R, Okishima K, Tomokuni Y. 2012. Flow experience and health-related quality of life in community dwelling elderly Japanese. *Nurs Health Sci* 14(1): 52–57.

Chapter 5

The Flow Experience and Tolerance of Ambiguity

Abstract

This chapter introduces the relationship between flow and tolerance of ambiguity. I first present an overview of tolerance of ambiguity. Next, I introduce a method of measuring tolerance of ambiguity. Finally, I explore the relationship between the quality of the flow experience and tolerance of ambiguity.

Tolerance of Ambiguity

One may experience ambiguous situations in life. For example, when first visiting an unfamiliar place, one may not know the appropriate behavior for that setting. When one takes a test, one does not immediately know the results. Some people enjoy these ambiguous situations. Individual differences in how much one can cognitively cope with such vague situations is called tolerance of ambiguity [1]. Previous studies have demonstrated that tolerance of ambiguity is associated with well-being [2], creativity [3], lower stress levels [4], and risk-taking behavior [5]. Because of this, I considered it a characteristic of a positive individual.

Here, I introduce a psychological health-related measurement for tolerance of ambiguity [1]. This scale was created in reference to the measurement of tolerance of ambiguity (MAT) [6]. It is composed of 24 items (using a five-point scale), and is easy to use because the number of items is smaller than the MAT. Higher scores reflect a higher level of tolerance. This measure had depression and negative significant correlation [1].

Quality of the Flow Experience and Tolerance of Ambiguity

I introduce below the relationship between flow and tolerance of ambiguity [7]. Flow was measured with the Flow Experience Checklist [8], and tolerance of ambiguity was assessed with the psychological health-related measure of tolerance of ambiguity [1]. The participants gathered in a lecture room, and questionnaires were distributed to them, which were completed after the authors explained the questionnaires in detail. The authors immediately collected the questionnaires once the participants had completed them. This survey was conducted at the end of the lecture. Study participants were a convenience sample of healthy college students (N = 68: 44 male and 24 female). The mean age of the sample was 22.6 years (SD = 4.6).

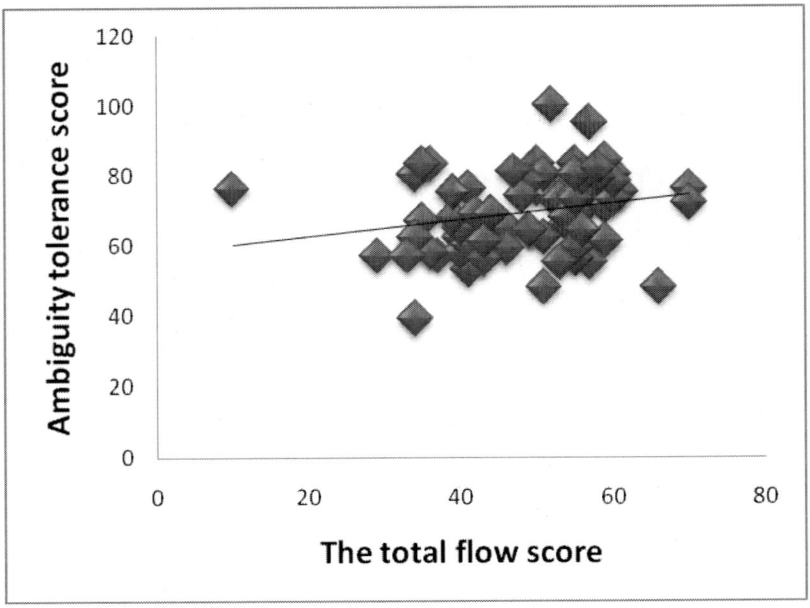

Figure 1. Correlations between tolerance of ambiguity score and the total score.

The mean for the Flow Experience Checklist was 4.51 ± 1.41 for frequency of flow experience and 48.54 ± 10.5 for quality of flow experience. MAT was 69.31 ± 11.23.

Correlations between the tolerance of ambiguity and the total flow scores are shown in Figure 1. The tolerance of ambiguity score showed a significant positive correlation with the total flow score. The total flow score indicates the quality of the flow experience. These findings suggest that total immersion in an activity enables one to withstand ambiguous situations, an ability that may reduce negative emotions in daily life.

This chapter is based on a study first reported in Hirao K, Kobayashi R, Yabuwaki K. 2012. Association of cognitive judgment and shyness with frequency and quality of flow experience. Psychol Res Behav Manag. 5:159-62.

References

[1] Masuda S.1988. Effects of tolerance of ambiguity on the psychological stress process. *Bulletin of the Faculty of Education Ibaraki University* 47:151–163.

[2] Yakhnich L, Ben-Zur H. 2008. Personal resources, appraisal, and coping in the adaptation process of immigrants from the Former Soviet Union. *Am J Orthopsychiatry*. Apr;78(2):152–62.

[3] Zenasni F, Besancon M, Lubart t. 2008. Creativity and Tolerance of Ambiguity: An Empirical Study. *Journal of Creative Behavior* v42 n1 p61–73

[4] Caulfield M, Andolsek K, Grbic D, Roskovensky L. 2014. Tolerance of ambiguity of students matriculating to U.S. medical schools. *Acad Med.* Nov;89(11):1526–32.

[5] Tymula A, Rosenberg Belmaker LA, Roy AK, Ruderman L, Manson K, Glimcher PW, Levy I. 2012 Adolescents' risk-taking behavior is driven by tolerance of ambiguity. *Proc Natl Acad Sci USA*. 2012 Oct 16;109(42):17135–40.

[6] Norton RW. 1975. Measurement of tolerance of ambiguity. *J Pers Assess*.39(6):607–619.

[7] Hirao K, Kobayashi R, Yabuwaki K.2012. Association of cognitive judgment and shyness with frequency and quality of flow experience. *Psychol Res Behav Manag*. 5:159–62.

[8] Ishimura I. 2009. Psychological study on enhancing factors and positive functions of flow experiences. Ibaraki: Doctoral thesis from the School of Comprehensive Human Sciences, University of Tsukuba.

Chapter 6

The Flow Experience and Shyness

Abstract

This chapter introduces the relationship between flow and shyness. I first present an overview of shyness. Next, I introduce a method of measuring shyness.

Finally, I explain the relationship between the frequency of flow experience and shyness.

Shyness

Shyness is a social anxiety that interferes with the ability to socialize effectively with others [1]. It can become a mental handicap and a social and personal disadvantage. [2–4]. Thus, shyness can be a factor that reduces the quality of life, life satisfaction, and happiness. Those with a high tendency towards shyness can easily suffer from behavioral obstacles in interpersonal relationships. A recent study suggested a positive relationship between shyness and problematic Internet use among adolescents [5]. In contrast, another recent study suggested a positive role of shyness [6], specifically, that the positive expression of shyness is a negative influence on anxiety [6].

In a behavioral study of interpersonal exchanges involving shy people, shy individuals were found to look away upon seeing the face of another person

[7]. A previous study suggested a relationship between shyness and love styles [8]. Shyness also affects other important aspects of life.

The Measurement of Shyness

Some standards of measuring shyness exist [9–11]; this chapter uses the Shyness Scale [12], described below.

Shyness Scale [12]

This scale was based on the Social Reticence Scale [11]. This scale consists of 19 items scored on a five-point scale. A high score reflects a high tendency towards shyness. Moreover, the top 25%-scoring group may assume a wider interpersonal distance than the lowest 25%-scoring group [12].

Frequency of Flow and Shyness

I introduce below the relationship between the flow experience and shyness [13]. Flow experiences were assessed with the Flow Experience Checklist [14], and shyness was assessed with the Shyness Scale [12]. Study participants were 68 college students (mean age: 22.6 years (SD = 4.6); 44 male and 24 female). The mean for the Flow Experience Checklist was 4.51 ± 1.41 for frequency of flow experience and 48.54 ± 10.5 for quality of flow experience. The mean for the Shyness Scale was 53.6 ± 14.78. Shyness scores were significantly negatively correlated with the frequency of flow scores, suggesting a correlation between a low frequency of flow and high shyness. Because interpersonal tension is high in shy individuals, it is possible that their worries about people in the surrounding environment could prevent flow. Flow requires extreme concentration. Thus, the social anxiety associated with shyness could obstruct a flow experience. Highly shy individuals are likely to agree with the items "When I perform a task, I recognize my ability is low" or "When I perform a task, I recognize the challenge level as high." Therefore, it is difficult for them to enter the flow state.

This chapter is based on a study first reported in Hirao K, Kobayashi R, Yabuwaki K.2012. Association of cognitive judgment and shyness with frequency and quality of flow experience. *Psychol Res Behav Manag*. 5:159-62

References

[1] Jones WH, Russell D. 1982. The Social Reticence Scale: An objective instrument to measure shyness. *J Pers Assess*. 46(6):629–31.

[2] Zimbardo PG, Pilkonis PA, and Norwood RM. 1974: *The silent prison of shyness,* Office of Naval Research Technical Report Z- 17, Stanford University.

[3] Zimbardo PG, Pilkonis PA, and Norwood RM. 1975.The social disease called shyness. *Psychology Today*, 8, 68–72.

[4] Zimbardo PG. 1977.: *Shyness: what it is, what to do about it.* Massachusetts: Addison-Wesley Publishing Company.

[5] Huan VS, Ang RP, Chong WH, Chye S. 2014. The impact of shyness on problematic internet use: the role of loneliness. *J Psychol*. Nov-Dec;148(6):699–715.

[6] Colonnesi C, Napoleone E, Bögels SM. 2014. Positive and negative expressions of shyness in toddlers: Are they related to anxiety in the same way? *J Pers Soc Psychol.* 106(4):624–37.

[7] Wang Q, Hu C, Short LA, Fu G. 2012.The influence of shyness on the scanning of own- and other-race faces in adults. PLoS One. 7(12):e52203.

[8] Erwin PG, Pressler SJ. 2011. Love styles, shyness, and patterns of emotional self-disclosure. *Psychol Rep*. 108(3):737–42.

[9] Watson D., Friend R, 1969. Measurement of social-evaluative anxiety. *Journal of Consulting and Clinical Psychology* 33(4) 448–457.

[10] Chee JM and Buss AH. 1981. Shyness and sociability. *Journal of Personality and Social Psychology* 41(2) 330–339.

[11] Jones WH, Russell D. 1982. The Social Reticence Scale: an objective instrument to measure shyness. *J Pers Assess*. 46(6):629–631.

[12] Sakurai S, Sakurai T. 1991. Daigakusei-you shyness syakudo no nihongo-ban no sakusei to datousei no kentou [Construction of Japanese version of Shyness Scale for college students]. *Bulletin of Nara University Education*. 40(1):235–243.

[13] Hirao K, Kobayashi R, Yabuwaki K. 2012. Association of cognitive judgment and shyness with frequency and quality of flow experience. *Psychol Res Behav Manag*. 5:159–62.

[14] Ishimura I. 2009. Psychological study on enhancing factors and positive functions of flow experiences. Ibaraki: Doctoral thesis from the School of Comprehensive Human Sciences, University of Tsukuba.

Chapter 7

The Flow Experience and Feelings of Optimism

Abstract

This chapter introduces the relationship between flow and optimism. I first present an overview of optimism. Next, I introduce a method of measuring optimism. Finally, I explain the relationship between quality of flow and feelings of optimism.

Optimism

Optimism is a tendency to expect future positive results [1]. An optimistic explanatory style towards positive events involves three qualities: internally oriented (involving a relationship with oneself), permanence, and universality (an individual acts on every case) [1]. An optimist is an individual with such an explanatory style.

In the United States, optimistic individuals tend to belong to high-status occupations and have high incomes by middle age [2]. This suggests that optimism is associated with economic success. Stroke survivors and their family caregivers with lower optimism had higher levels of depressive symptoms [3]. This suggests that high optimism is associated with low depressive symptoms. Optimism in adolescents in the Netherlands was found to be affected by genetics [4], suggesting a need to consider genetic factors in optimistic studies. Another study also showed a clear influence of optimism on recovery after total hip replacement in the first 3 months after surgery [5], suggesting that optimism positively impacts physical functional recovery. Optimism was also found to have a protective factor in mental health among the unemployed [6]. Hair cortisol, which reflects chronic stress, was also found to have a significant inverse association with dispositional optimism among adolescents [7], suggesting that high optimism is associated with low chronic stress.

A positive correlation was also found between optimism and life quality in morphea patients [8], suggesting that optimism has a positive impact on quality of life in dermatological diseases. Psychological interventions for optimism were also recommended to enhance the quality of life of breast cancer patients [9].

Measurement of Feelings of Optimism [11]

The Life Orientation Test is widely used to measure optimism [10].

This chapter used a Japanese language version of the Life Orientation Test [11]. This scale comprises 12 items scored on a 5-point scale. Higher scores reflect higher levels of optimism. This scale is considered useful for clarifying associations between optimism and mental health [11].

The Quality of Flow and Feelings of Optimism

I introduce below the relationship between flow and optimism [12]. In this chapter, flow experiences were assessed with the Flow Experience Checklist [13], optimism was assessed with the Life Orientation Test [11]. Study participants were a convenience sample of healthy college students (N = 68: 44 male and 24 female). The mean age of the sample was 22.6 years (SD = 4.6). The mean for the Flow Experience Checklist was 4.51 ± 1.41 for frequency of flow experience and 48.54 ± 10.5 for quality of flow experience. Life Orientation Test was 8.97 ± 2.44 for self-feeling optimistic. In the logistic regression analysis, the Feelings of Optimism score was not a predictor of quality of flow experience [12]. However, the optimism score was found to correlate positively with the total flow score (Figure 1). Optimistic individuals may also be able to take on high levels of challenge proactively. Thus, flow and optimism are central to a positive psychological state and evidence suggests they are mutually related.

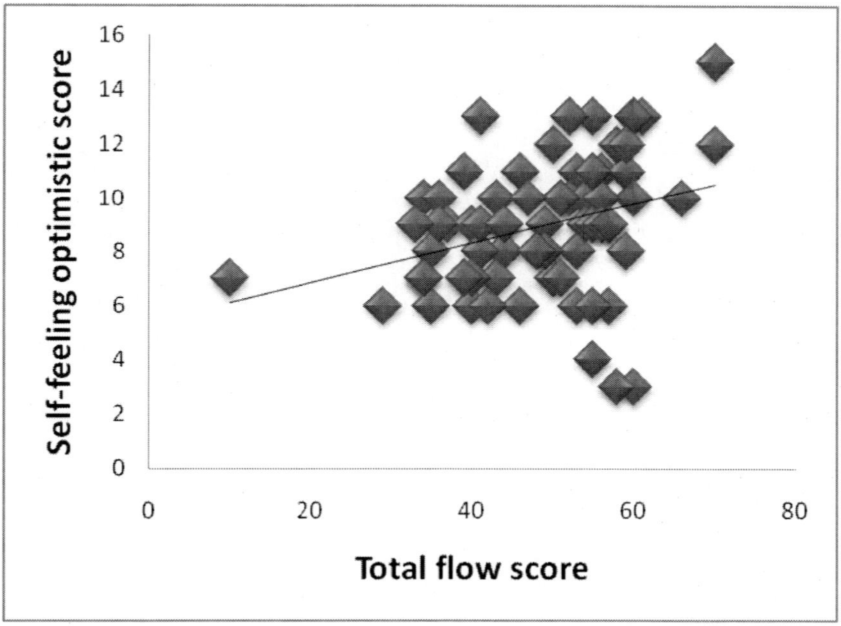

Figure 1. Correlations between optimism and the total flow scores.

This chapter is based on a study first reported in Hirao K, Kobayashi R, Yabuwaki K. 2012. Association of cognitive judgment and shyness with frequency and quality of flow experience. *Psychol Res Behav Manag*. 5:159-62

References

[1] Seligman, MEP. 1991. *Learned Optimism*, Alfred A. Knopf, New York.

[2] Boehm JK, Chen Y, Williams DR, Ryff C, Kubzansky LD.2015. Unequally distributed psychological assets: Are there social disparities in optimism, life satisfaction, and positive affect? *PLoS One*. 2015 Feb 11;10(2):e0118066.

[3] Chung ML, Bakas T, Plue LD, Williams LS. 2015. Effects of self-esteem, optimism, and perceived control on depressive symptoms in stroke survivor-spouse dyads. *J Cardiovasc Nurs.* [Epub ahead of print]

[4] Mavioğlu RN, Boomsma DI, Bartels M. 2015. Causes of individual differences in adolescent optimism: A study in Dutch twins and their siblings. *Eur Child Adolesc Psychiatry.* [Epub ahead of print]

[5] Balck F, Lippmann M, Jeszenszky C, Günther KP, Kirschner S. 2015. The influence of optimism on functionality after total hip replacement surgery. *J Health Psychol.* pii: 1359105314566256. [Epub ahead of print]

[6] Bilajac L, Marchesi VV, Tešić V, Rukavina T. 2014. Life satisfaction, optimism and social capital as predictors of mental health of the recipients of financial welfare from the state. *Psychiatr Danub.* Suppl 3:435–41.

[7] Milam J, Slaughter R, Verma G, McConnell R. 2014. Hair cortisol, perceived stress and dispositional optimism: A pilot study among adolescents. *J Trauma Stress Disord Treat.* 3(3):1000126.

[8] Szramka-Pawlak B, Dańczak-Pazdrowska A, Rzepa T, Szewczyk A, Sadowska-Przytocka A, Zaba R. 2014. Quality of life and optimism in patients with morphea. *Appl Res Qual Life* 9(4):863–870.

[9] Ha EH, Cho YK. 2014. The mediating effects of self-esteem and optimism on the relationship between quality of life and depressive symptoms of breast cancer patients. *Psychiatry Investig.* Oct;11(4):437–45.

[10] Scheier MF, Carver CS. 1985. Optimism, coping, and health: assessment and implications of generalized outcome expectancies. *Health Psychol.*;4(3):219–247.

[11] Nakamura H. 2000. *Individual differences of psychological characteristics in the face-to-face setting.* Tokyo: Brain Shuppan.

[12] Hirao K, Kobayashi R, Yabuwaki K. 2012. Association of cognitive judgment and shyness with frequency and quality of flow experience. *Psychol Res Behav Manag.* 5:159–62.

[13] Ishimura I. 2009. Psychological study on enhancing factors and positive functions of flow experiences. Ibaraki: Doctoral thesis from the School of Comprehensive Human Sciences, University of Tsukuba.

Chapter 8

The Flow Experience and Self-Disgust

Abstract

This chapter introduces the relationship between flow experience and self-disgust. I first present an overview of self-disgust. Next, I introduced a method of measuring the self-disgust. Finally, I explain the relationship between frequency of flow and self-disgust.

Self-Disgust

Self-disgust is defined as a negative feeling related to a lack of confidence [1]. Self-disgust is self-hatred [2]. There may be differences of degree, but most people have some self-disgust. In other words, self-disgust involves strong negative feelings. For youth in particular, becoming aware of one's negative traits while gaining self-awareness can lead to sensitivity [2]. In this way, self-disgust is an important emotion in the process of human maturation.

However, self-disgust is not necessarily a positive mental state. Previous studies have suggested that self-disgust mediates the relation between depressive symptoms and nonsuicidal self-injury and partially mediates the relation between sexual abuse and nonsuicidal self-injury among college students [3]. Another study suggested that self-disgust is higher in those with mental disorders than in healthy subjects [4], and self-disgust is related to specific psychological problems [4]. Self-disgust has also been described as a consuming negative psychological phenomenon associated with depression, eating disorders, physical appearance, interpersonal relationships, and self-persecution [5]. A longitudinal study suggested that self-disgust is a predictor of depressive symptoms [6].

Measurement of Self-Disgust [2]

Here, I introduce the Self-Disgust Scale [2] used in this chapter [7]. The Self-Disgust Scale is composed of one factor and contains 21 items scored on a five-point scale. A high score reflects high self-disgust. The self-disgust score was significantly negatively correlated with the self-esteem score [2].

Frequency of Flow and Self-Disgust

In this chapter, flow experiences were measured with the Flow Experience Checklist [8] and self-disgust was measured with the Self-Disgust Scale [2].

I distributed a questionnaire to the participants in a lecture room and explained the questionnaire in detail. The questionnaires were immediately collected from the participants on completion. This questionnaire survey was conducted after a regular lecture. Study participants were 142 college students (mean age, 20.09 ± 1.24 years; 85 males and 57 females. The frequency of flow experiences was 4.7 ± 1.17, and the duration of the activity (h/week) was 10.36 ± 8.94. The quality of the flow experience was 46.27 ± 6.66. The Self-disgust Scale score was 66.03 ± 22.03. The self-disgust score was significantly and negatively correlated with the frequency of flow score, suggesting that individuals with high self-disgust have difficulty experiencing flow. It may be hard to feel motivated to tackle challenging tasks in a mental state dominated by negative emotions. Individuals with high self-disgust tend to compare themselves to others and often regard themselves as inferior.

Another reflection of high self-disgust is perfectionism; it is healthier to complete tasks reasonably than to feel pressured to complete them perfectly, since perfect human beings do not exist. It is important for individuals to be able to forgive themselves for not being perfect. The frequency of flow may increase in individuals who consciously decrease their perfectionist tendencies.

This chapter is based on a study first reported in Hirao K, Kobayashi R.2013. The relationship between self-disgust, guilt, and flow experience among Japanese undergraduates. *Neuropsychiatr Dis Treat*. 9:985-8.

References

[1] Satoh Y. 2001. Self-Disgust and self-affirmation in university students. *Jpn J Educ Psychol.* 49(3):347–358.

[2] Mizuma R.1996. The construction of self-disgust scale. *Kyoiku Shinrigaku Kenkyu*. 44(3):296–302.

[3] Smith NB, Steele AM, Weitzman ML, Trueba AF, Meuret AE.2015. Investigating the Role of Self-Disgust in Nonsuicidal Self-Injury. *Arch Suicide Res.* 19(1):60–74.

[4] Ille R, Schöggl H, Kapfhammer HP, Arendasy M, Sommer M, Schienle A. 2014. Self-disgust in mental disorders – symptom-related or disorder-specific? *Compr Psychiatry.* 55(4):938–43.

[5] Powell PA, Overton PG, Simpson J. 2014. The revolting self: an interpretative phenomenological analysis of the experience of self-disgust in females with depressive symptoms. *J Clin Psychol.* 70(6):562–78.

[6] Powell PA, Simpson J, Overton PG. 2013.When disgust leads to dysphoria: a three-wave longitudinal study assessing the temporal relationship between self-disgust and depressive symptoms. *Cogn Emot.* 27(5):900–13.

[7] Hirao K, Kobayashi R.2013. The relationship between self-disgust, guilt, and flow experience among Japanese undergraduates. *Neuropsychiatr Dis Treat*. 9:985–8.

[8] Ishimura I. 2009. *Psychological study on enhancing factors and positive functions of flow experiences*. Ibaraki: Doctoral thesis from the School of Comprehensive Human Sciences, University of Tsukuba.

Chapter 9

The Flow Experience and Guilt

Abstract

This chapter introduces the relationship between flow and guilt. I first present an overview of guilt. Next, I introduce a method for measuring guilt. Then, I explain the relationship between duration of activity and guilt. Finally, I explain the relationship between quality of flow experience and guilt.

Guilt

Guilt means disappointment or regret about having done something wrong. It involves twinges of conscience and is considered negative [1]. Guilt is among the feelings that everybody experiences. Because it involves negative emotions about the self, it is a painful in nature. Those who experience a sense of guilt are motivated to compensate for their misdeeds [2]. A guilty person's self-evaluation as having been failed results from focusing on the self or the specific features or acts leading to failure [3]. However, a sense of guilt is not in itself self-destructive and can be considered a helpful emotion for motivating changes in behavior [3].

Below, I introduce recent research on guilt. A previous study has suggested that guilt is not associated with hostile irritability in girls showing greater symptoms of borderline personality disorder [4]. Another study suggested that provision of caring is associated with decreased guilt among sufferers of severe Post-Traumatic Stress Disorder [5]. Other research suggested that patients experiencing chronic pain patients had higher guilt levels than normal population (controls) [6]. Trauma-related guilt has also been found to be related to mental health following mass trauma [7].

Measurement of Guilt [10, 11]

Scales for measuring guilt include the Personal Feelings Questionnaire [8], the Guilt Inventory [9], and the Situational Guilt Inventory [10, 11]. Here, I introduce the Situational Guilt Inventory [10, 11], used in the research for this chapter.

The Situational Guilt Inventory is composed of 31 items, each scored on a four-point scale. This measure examines the tendency to feel guilt. A high score on the scale indicated a high tendency to experience guilt.

The Situational Guilt Inventory score showed a significant positive correlation with depression and anxiety as well as with neuroticism, conscientiousness, and agreeableness. The score also exhibited a significantly negative correlation with lying behaviors.

Duration of Activity and Guilt

This chapter examines the relationship between guilt and flow [12]. Flow experiences were measured with the Flow Experience Checklist [13], and guilt was measured with the Situational Guilt Inventory [10, 11].

This study was conducted in a convenience sample of 142 university students (mean age, 20.09 ± 1.24 years; 85 males and 57 females). The frequency of flow experiences was 4.7 ± 1.17, and the duration of the activity (h/week) was 10.36 ± 8.94. The quality of the flow experience was 46.27 ± 6.66. The Situational Guilt Inventory score was 102.71 ± 12.32.

The Situational Guilt Inventory score showed a significant positive correlation with the duration of activities. Here duration of activities indicates the time spent on important activities in everyday life. Thus, an individual with a strong sense of guilt spends more time on important activities than the one without guilt. This result could be interpreted as a negative aspect of flow, if guilt is considered a negative feeling. It could also be interpreted to mean that long times spent on important activities are a compensatory action to correct any misdeeds that have resulted in guilt [14]. Generally, because agreeable activities trigger flow, such activities are performed often, and consequently, significant amounts of time are spent on them. However, another possible reason for dedicating significant time to activities could be negative feelings such as guilt.

Quality of Flow and Guilt

The Situational Guilt Inventory score showed a significant positive correlation with the quality of the flow experience. In other words, individuals with strong senses of guilt experienced high quality of flow experience. Conversely, individuals who devoted much time to specific activities could have felt significant guilt. Because of this guilt, one might choose to stay immersed in activities to avoid feeling dominated by guilt. In other words, there is a possibility that the flow could be facilitated by negative emotions, since surrounding distractions are not a concern to a person in the flow state, who is deeply concentrating on the activity at hand.

This chapter is based on a study first reported in Hirao K, Kobayashi R. 2013. The relationship between self-disgust, guilt, and flow experience among Japanese undergraduates. *Neuropsychiatr Dis Treat.* 9:985-8.

References

[1] Tangney, J. P., Wagner, P. E., Fletcher, C., & Gramzow, R. 1992. Shamed into anger? The relation of shame and guilt to anger and self-reported aggression. *Journal of Personality and Social Psychology*, 62, 669–675.

[2] Tangney JP, Burggraf SA, Wagner PE. 1995. Shame-proneness, guilt-proneness, and psychological symptoms. In: Tangney JP, Fischer KW, editors. *Self-conscious emotions: The psychology of shame, guilt, embarrassment, and pride*. New York, NY: Guilford Press, 343–367.

[3] Lewis, HB. 1992. *Shame: The exposed self.* New York: Free Press.

[4] Scott LN, Stepp SD, Hallquist MN, Whalen DJ, Wright AG, Pilkonis PA. 2015. Daily shame and hostile irritability in adolescent girls with borderline personality disorder symptoms. *Personal Disord.* 6(1):53–63.

[5] Leifker FR, White KH, Blandon AY, Marshall AD. 2015. Posttraumatic stress disorder symptoms impact the emotional experience of intimacy during couple discussions. *J Anxiety Disord.* 29:119–27.

[6] Turner-Cobb JM, Michalaki M, Osborn M. 2015. Self-conscious emotions in patients suffering from chronic musculoskeletal pain: A brief report. *Psychol Health* 30(4):495–501.

[7] Aakvaag HF, Thoresen S, Wentzel-Larsen T, Røysamb E, Dyb G. 2014. Shame and guilt in the aftermath of terror: the Utøya Island study. *J Trauma Stress.* 27(5):618–21.

[8] Harder DH, Zalma A. 1990.Two promising shame and guilt scales: A construct validity comparison. *J Pers Assess.* 55(3–4):729–45.

[9] Kugler KJ, Warren H. 1992. On conceptualizing and assessing guilt. *Journal of Personality and Social Psychology* 62(2) 318–327.

[10] Arimitsu K. 2002. Structure of guilt eliciting situations in Japanese adolescents. *Shinrigaku Kenkyu* 73(2):148–156.

[11] Arimitsu K. 2006. Guilt, shame/embarrassment, and empathy. *Shinrigaku Kenkyu* 77(2):97–104.

[12] Hirao K, Kobayashi R. 2013. The relationship between self-disgust, guilt, and flow experience among Japanese undergraduates. *Neuropsychiatr Dis Treat.* 9:985–8.

[13] Ishimura I. 2009. Psychological study on enhancing factors and positive functions of flow experiences. Ibaraki: Doctoral thesis from the School of Comprehensive Human Sciences, University of Tsukuba

[14] Baumeister RF, Stillwell AM, Heatherton TF. 1994. Guilt: an interpersonal approach. *Psychol Bull.* 115(2):24367.

Chapter 10

The Flow Experience and Emotional Intelligence

Abstract

This chapter investigates the relationship between emotional intelligence (EI) and flow experience in daily life among adolescents. The results indicate a statistically significant positive correlation between EI and the flow experience. These findings suggest that the development of EI can facilitate flow in adolescents.

Introduction

Positive psychology is a scientific field that focuses on the virtues of positive personality, positive experiences, and their development [1]. Positive psychology has been found to help improve the mental health of adolescents [2]. In addition, flow and emotional intelligence (EI) both play central roles in positive psychology [2]. Flow is the positive mental state that occurs when a person is fully absorbed in a particular activity [3]. Previous studies have shown that flow is positively associated with decreased subjective stress [4] and health-related quality of life (QOL) [5] in adolescents. EI refers to the ability to evaluate one's emotions and those of others and to manage one's emotions to enhance performance [6]. Previous studies have also suggested that EI programs promote the mental health of adolescents [7].

Thus, flow and EI both contribute to the mental health of adolescents. However, research on the relationship between flow in daily life and EI in adolescents has been limited. Therefore, this chapter investigates the relationship between flow and EI in this demographic.

Methods

Participants in this cross-sectional study comprised 69 adolescents (42 males and 27 females ranging in age from 19 to 25 years (M = 20.35, SD = 1.08)) from a single college located in western Japan. All the participants were assured of their anonymity, and they provided their written informed consent. This chapter was approved by the institutional review board at Kibi International University in Okayama, Japan.

Measures

The Japanese translation of the Wong and Law [8] Emotional Intelligence Scale (J-WLEIS) was utilized to measure individual differences in EI [9]. This scale comprised 16 items (scored on a 7-point Likert scale) encompassing four factors: regulation of emotion; self-emotions appraisal; use of emotion; and others-emotions appraisal. In this case, higher scores reflected higher EI. The measure's reliability and validity has been previously established [9].

The Flow Experience Checklist (FEC) was applied to measure the frequency and degree of flow in daily life [10]. The FEC comprises one item measuring the frequency of flow experience and 10 items measuring the degree of flow experience (scored on a 7-point Likert scale). A higher score reflected a higher frequency and degree of flow experience. The reliability and validity of the FEC has been previously established [10].

Procedure

Information sheets describing the study and the checklist were distributed to the participants. The authors explained the checklist in detail, which the participants then completed during class periods.

Data Analysis

The relationship between the two continuous variables (J-WLEIS and FEC) was assessed with Pearson's partial correlation analysis, which was adjusted for age and gender. In addition, this correlation analysis was used to describe the strength and direction of the relationship between the variables. Because the P-value was <0.05, the difference between the two variables was statistically significant. All analyses were conducted using SPSS version 19 for Windows.

Results

The participants' characteristics are displayed in Table 1. The frequency of flow experiences was 4.99 ± 0.99, the degree of flow experience was 48.94 ± 8.29, and the J-WLEIS score was 68.81 ± 10.9. The correlation between the J-WLEIS and the FEC is displayed in Table 2. The J-WLEIS score was found to correlate with the degree of flow experience ($r = .35$, $p < 0.01$). Furthermore, regulation of emotion and self-emotions appraisal were found to correlate with the degree of flow experience ($r = .29$, $p < 0.05$ and $r = .35$, $p < 0.01$), while self-emotions appraisal was found to correlate with the frequency of flow experience ($r = .29$, $p < 0.05$).

Table 1. Characteristics of the participants

	Mean	SD
Age (years)	20.35	1.08
Gender (male/female)	42/27	
FEC		
Frequency of flow experience	4.99	0.99
Degree of flow experience	48.94	8.29
J-WLEIS		
Regulation of Emotion	16.36	4.07
Self-Emotions Appraisal	19.46	4.19
Use of Emotion	14.99	3.4
Others-Emotions Appraisal	18	2.89
J-WLEIS score	68.81	10.9

Note: FEC = Flow Experience Checklist.
J-WLEIS = Japanese Version of Wong and Law Emotional Intelligence Scale.

Table 2. Correlation between the J-WLEIS and the FEC

J-WLEIS	Regulation of Emotion	Self-Emotions Appraisal	Use of Emotion	Others'-Emotions Appraisal	J-WLEIS score
FEC					
Frequency of flow experience	0.13	0.29*	0.01	0.01	0.17
Degree of flow experience	0.29*	0.35**	0.18	0.2	0.35**

*p < 0.05, **p < 0.01.

Note: FEC = Flow Experience Checklist; J-WLEIS = Japanese Version of Wong and Law Emotional Intelligence Scale.

Partial correlations were adjusted for age and gender.

Discussion

The results indicate that EI (regulation of emotion and self-emotions appraisal) is related to the frequency and the degree of flow experience in daily life of adolescents. In addition, the highest degree of the regulation of emotion involves reaching a mental state in that one can control emotions [9]. According to Nakamura and Csikszentmihalyi [11], flow experiences provide "A sense that one can control one's actions, that is, a sense that one can in principle deal with the situation because one knows how to respond to whatever happens next." Thus, the regulation of emotion in EI is related to the degree of flow experience because both variables include this particular factor. Furthermore, self-emotions appraisal is a state in which one can better understand one's emotions [9]. Because the universal factors of flow include clear goals but unambiguous feedback, [11, 12] the present study finds that a better understanding of self-emotions is closely related to a good psychological state.

Finally, previous studies have suggested that flow experience includes a decrease in subjective stress [4], which is positively associated with mental QOL [5] and psychological tendencies [13, 14] in adolescents. In the present study, EI is associated with flow experience in adolescents. Although the findings of the current study provide an adequate basis for future research, there were some limitations. First, the sample size was small, and the study was conducted at a single point in time, which limited identification of the direction of causality between the variables. Moreover, because only basic demographic information was collected, such as age and gender, this also could have influenced the EI and flow experience in the study group. Therefore, further prospective and longitudinal research is required with a larger cohort to control for potential confounding factors.

References

[1] Duckworth AL, Steen TA, Seligman ME. 2005. Positive psychology in clinical practice. *Annu Rev Clin Psychol.* 1:629–651.

[2] Kelley TM. 2004. Positive psychology and adolescent mental health: False promise or true breakthrough? *Adolescence* 39(154):257–278.

[3] Csikszentmihalyi M, Csikszentmihalyi I. 1988. *Optimal experience: Psychological studies of flow in consciousness.* Cambridge: Cambridge University Press.

[4] Hirao K, Kobayashi R, Okishima K, Tomokuni Y, Yabuwaki K.2011 Influence of different intensities of brief flow experiences on subjective and objective stress. *Med Biol.* 155:713–720.

[5] Hirao K, Kobayashi R, Okishima K, Tomokuni Y. 2011. Influence of flow experience during daily life on health-related quality of life and salivary amylase activity in Japanese college students. *JJOMT* 59:13–18.

[6] Law KS, Wong CS, Song LJ. 2004 The construct and criterion validity of emotional intelligence and its potential utility for management studies. *J Appl Psychol.* 89(3):483–496.

[7] Ruiz-Aranda D, Castillo R, Salguero JM, Cabello R, Fernández-Berrocal P, Balluerka N. 2012. Short- and midterm effects of emotional intelligence training on adolescent mental health. *J Adolesc Health* 51(5):462–467.

[8] Wong CS, Law KS. 2002. The effects of leader and follower emotional intelligence on performance and attitude: An exploratory study. *Leadersh Q.* 13:243–274.

[9] Toyota H, Yamamoto K.2011. Development of a Japanese Version of the Wong and Law Emotional Intelligence Scale. *Bulletin of Center for Educational Research and Development.* 20:7–12.

[10] Ishimura I.2008. *Psychological study of enhancing factors and positive functions of flow experiences.* Tsukuba, Ibaraki: University of Tsukuba. Doctoral thesis.

[11] Nakamura J, Csikszentmihalyi M. 2002. *The concept of flow*. In: Snyder CR, Lopez SJ, Eds. *Handbook of positive psychology*. New York: Oxford University Press 89–105.

[12] Csikszentmihalyi M.1990. *Flow: The psychology of optimal experience*. New York: Harper and Row.

[13] Hirao K, Kobayashi R. 2013. The relationship between self-disgust, guilt, and flow experience among Japanese undergraduates. *Neuropsychiatr Dis Treat*. 9:985–988.

[14] Hirao K, Kobayashi R, Yabuwaki K. 2012. Association of cognitive judgment and shyness with frequency and quality of flow experience. *Psychol Res Behav Manag*. 5:159–162.

Chapter 11

Changes in Flow Experience

Abstract

This chapter introduces changes in flow experience among occupational therapy students, with a focus on differences by gender. I first present a summary of change in flow experience. Then, I describe the changes in flow experience of all participants and the changes in flow experience in female and male participants.

Introduction

Do frequency and the degree of the flow experience change? Generally, the flow model is to promote the development of individual ability [1]. Therefore, the flow experience is believed to be changeable rather than fixed. Previous studies have suggested that high school students who continued gaining expertise in an activity for four years experienced more flow [2].

I introduce a follow-up study of flow experience in occupational therapy students below [3]. In this chapter, flow experiences were assessed with the Flow Experience Checklist [4]. Occupational therapists were chosen as subjects for this chapter because maintaining a stable quality of life is important for those in the profession: One of their key professional responsibilities is promoting their clients' quality of life, and they would not be able to provide interventions or evaluations effectively while in a negative mental state.

In December 2012, I prospectively recruited 97 occupational therapy students from the Department of Occupational Therapy, Kibi International University, Okayama, Japan. I included 87 occupational therapy students in the analysis.

The dataset included 87 occupational therapy students, of which 75 participated in the assessment for one year (follow-up rate, 86.2%). The mean age at baseline of 45 male and 30 female occupational therapy students was 19.59 ± 1.1 (range 18–24) years.

The Wilcoxon test was used to compare the Flow Experience Checklist at baseline (December 2012) with that after one year (December 2013). All analyses were the level of significance was defined as 5%.

Changes in Flow Experience in All and Female Participants

Changes in the frequency of flow experience for all participants are shown in Figure 1. Baseline was 4.69 ± 1.13. After one year, it was 4.49±1.12. This result suggests that the frequency of flow did not change over a single year in the participants. Figure 2 shows changes in the quality of flow among all participants. Baseline was 46.91±5.98. After one year it was 47.38±7.27. These findings suggest that quality of flow experience did not change over a single year, either.

The changes in frequency and quality of flow among female participants are shown in Figures 3 and 4, respectively. Frequency of flow experience of baseline was 4.37 ± 1.25. After one year was 4.50 ± 1.20. Quality of flow experience of baseline was 46.77 ± 5.07. After one year was 47.94 ± 7.27. These findings also suggest that neither frequency nor quality of flow changed within a year among female participants. Changes in quality of flow among female participants are shown in Figure 4. In other words, without intervention, flow experience did not change. This can be interpreted to mean the frequency and quality of the flow experience is steadily maintained in daily life. Although this result can be interpreted negatively by stating that lack of increase in the frequency and quality of flow experience may indicate no further personal growth. Because occupational therapy students are in the process of becoming occupational therapists, their flow experiences should be promoted; thus, it can be said that the result obtained was not in line with the expectation.

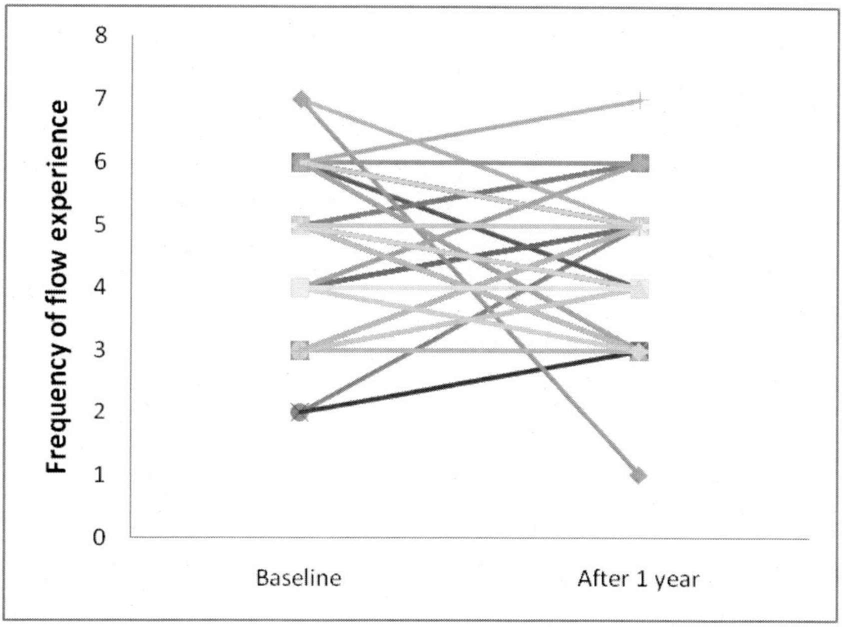

Figure 1. Changes in frequency of flow among all participants.

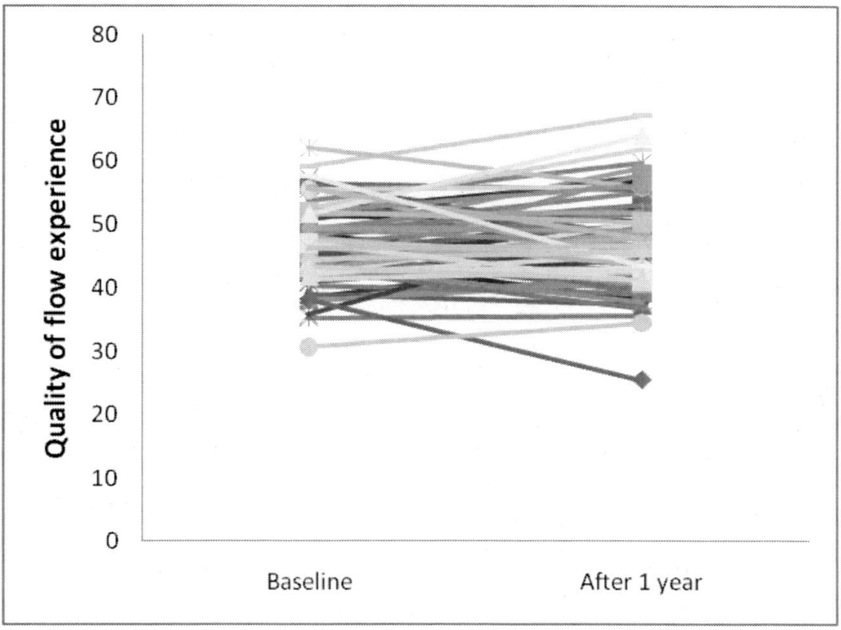

Figure 2. Changes in quality of flow among all participants.

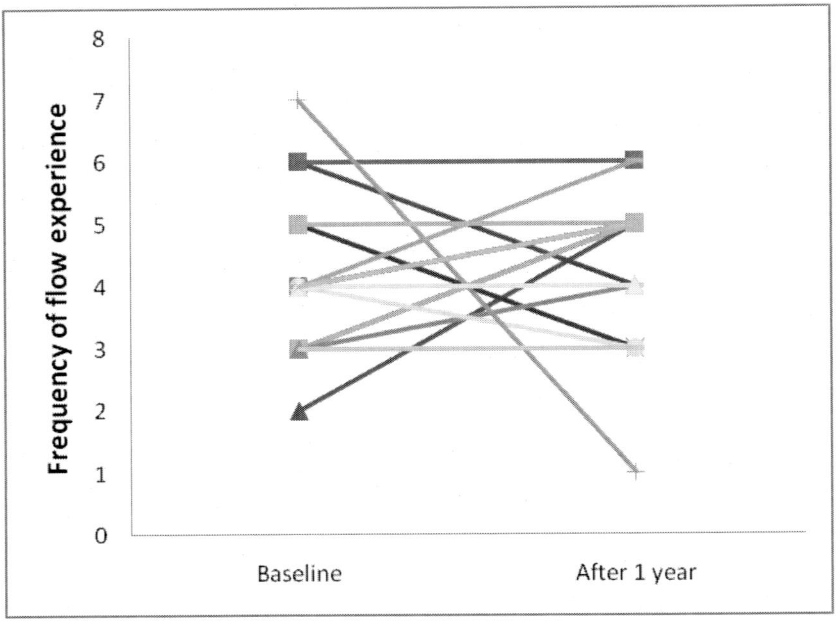

Figure 3. Changes in frequency of flow among female participants.

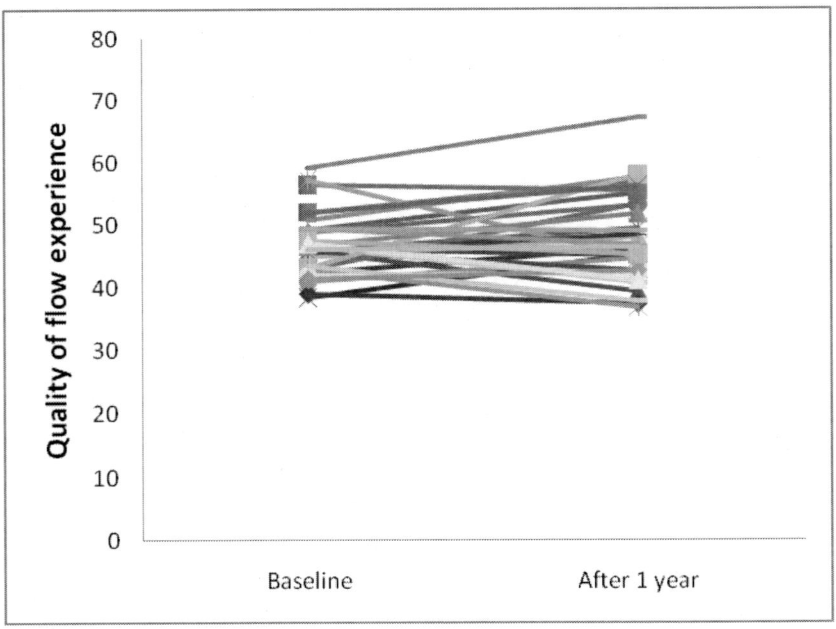

Figure 4.Changes in quality of flow experience among female participants.

Changes in Flow Experience in Male Participants

Changes in frequency of flow among male participants are shown in Figure 5, which shows that the frequency of flow decreased over a span of a year. Frequency of flow experience of baseline was 4.91 ± 1.00. After one year was 4.49 ± 1.08. Figure 6 shows the changes in the quality of flow among male participants and exhibits that the quality of flow experience did not change over a single year. Quality of flow experience of baseline was 47.00 ± 6.57. After one year was 47.01 ± 7.33. Therefore, active intervention is recommended to augment the frequency of flow in male participants. From a teacher's perspective, male occupational therapy students appear lazier than their female counterparts. As a result of lazy life, it is often results in translocation family to repeaters and other departments. Therefore, it is necessary to pay particular attention to male occupational therapy students.

This chapter is based on a study first reported in Hirao K. 2014.Changes in flow experience among occupational therapy students: A 1-year longitudinal study. *J Educ Eval Health Prof.* 7;11:14.

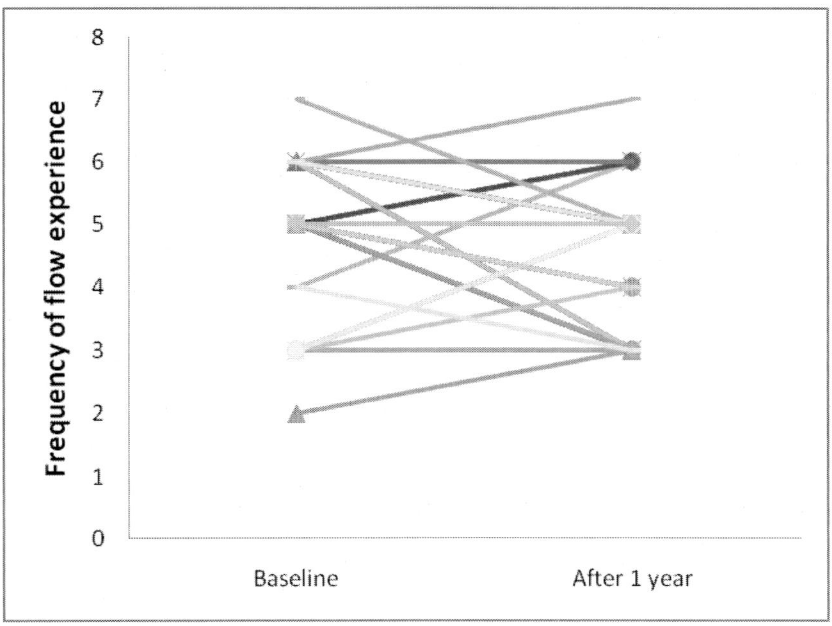

Figure 5. Changes in frequency of flow experience among male participants.

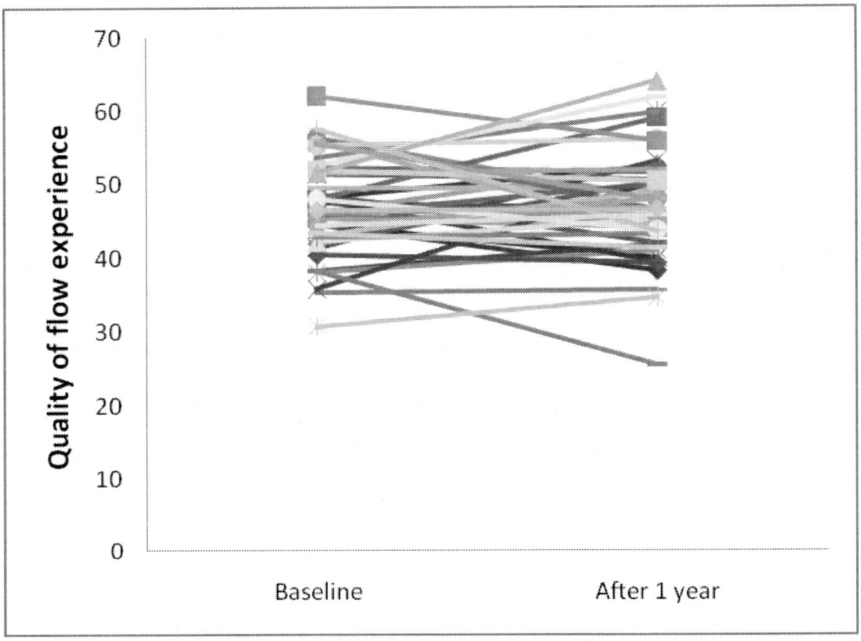

Figure 6. Changes in quality of flow experience among male participants.

References

[1] Nakamura J, Csikszentmihalyi M. 2002. The concept of flow, *Handbook of Positive Psychology*. New York: Oxford University Press.

[2] Csikszentmihalyi M, Rathunde K, Whalen S. 1993. *Talented teenagers: The roots of success and failure*. New York: Cambridge University Press.

[3] Hirao K. 2014. Changes in flow experience among occupational therapy students: A 1-year longitudinal study. *J Educ Eval Health Prof*. 2014 7;11:14.

[4] Ishimura I. 2009. *Psychological study on enhancing factors and positive functions of flow experiences*. Ibaraki: Doctoral thesis from the School of Comprehensive Human Sciences, University of Tsukuba.

Chapter 12

Autotelic Personality and Feelings of Inferiority

Abstract

This chapter compares feelings of inferiority in three groups: autotelic personality (AP), average (AV), or non-autotelic personality (NAP). I first present an overview of AP. Then, I introduce a method of measuring AP and provide an overview of feelings of inferiority. Next, I introduce a method of measuring feelings of inferiority. Finally, I show that feelings of inferiority are significantly lower in the AP group than in the NAP group.

Autotelic Personality

Autotelic personality (AP) is defined as a tendency to spend more time in the flow state [1]. In other words, those with AP work not for profit or reward but easily find joy and pleasure in their actions. Individuals with AP engage in work with a degree of difficulty slightly above their ability and immerse themselves fully in such work environments. AP individuals are able to concentrate on and enjoy activities that others dismiss as unimportant, such as riding a train or watching TV.

AP is associated with long-term academic success [2], personal innovativeness [3], self-efficacy and control [3], and satisfaction [4, 5].

The Flow Experience Checklist was used to measure AP [7]. Diagnosis of AP was based on previously reported methods [8]. Participants cited five important activities in everyday life. The number of flow experiences for each activity was determined from their "challenge to goals" and "confidence in skills" responses on the checklist. Using the mean values with a margin of ±1 SD of the number of flow activities, three groups were classified according to their AP characteristics and number of flow activities: AP, AV, or NAP.

Feelings of Inferiority

Feelings of inferiority indicate the sense that one is inferior to others [9]. Many people experience feelings of inferiority. For example, the home environment can prompt feelings of inferiority. From being scolded by one's parents in childhood as, for example, "an idiot," could cause a sense of inferiority. If such memories are retained, they can impact one's adulthood and cause a continued inferiority complex. Those whose self-evaluations are based on public opinion are also considered prone to feelings of inferiority. Because such people have no personal standards for themselves, they solely rely on external value judgments.

Feelings of inferiority are thought to be associated with cultural, social, and minority issues [10], and self-harm [11]. Patients with atopic dermatitis showed significantly higher scores for feelings of inferiority than those with psoriasis [12]. Participants with long-term depression reported feelings of inferiority significantly more often than participants with episodic major depressive episodes [13]. Feelings of inferiority were found to be the main sources of suicidal ideation in patients with schizophrenia [14]. Feelings of inferiority were also associated with suicidal ideation and suicide attempts among youth in the United States [15].

The Inferiority Feeling Scale [9] used in this chapter's research contains 50 items, each scored on a five-point scale. This scale has eight subscales (weakness in associating with the opposite sex, poor grades in school, low levels of home satisfaction, poor ability to make friends, poor performance in sports, "bad" personality, lack of social skills, and poor perceptions of bodily attractiveness). On this scale, higher scores indicated stronger feelings of inferiority.

Comparison of Feelings of Inferiority in the Three Groups (AP, AV, or NAP) [6]

Study participants were a convenience sample of healthy college students (N = 148: male = 88 and female = 60). The mean age of the sample was 20.05 ± 1.24 years. The χ^2 test, and one-way analysis of variance (ANOVA) was performed for the three groups (NAP, AV, and AP) using the dependent variables of age, sex, score on the Inferiority Feeling Scale, and score of each subscale. Tukey's test was used for multiple comparisons.

Using the mean values with a margin of ±1SD (mean = 1.37, SD = 1.29) of the number of flow activities, three groups were classified according to AP characteristics. Participants were classified into these groups by the number of flow activities reported: 3+ for AP (n = 28, 18.9%), 1–2 for AV (n = 72, 48.6%), 0 for NAP (n = 48, 32.4%). The results of $\chi 2$ test and one-way ANOVA did not show significant difference between the three groups with respect to gender or age.

Figure 1 compares the total scores for each of the three groups on the scale. Total average score was NAP (2.92±0.62), AV (2.59±0.77), and AP (2.41±0.91). Weakness in associating with the opposite sex average score was NAP (2.81±1.1), AV (2.59±1.11), and AP (2.42±1.47). Poor grades in school average score was NAP (3.6±0.95), AV (3.52±1.08), and AP (3.43±1.24). Poor performance in sports average score was NAP (2.77 ± 1.13), AV (2.52 ± 1.13), and AP (2.28 ± 1.19). Low levels of home satisfaction average score was NAP (1.88 ± 0.76), AV (1.65 ± 0.62), and AP (1.62 ± 0.63). "Bad" personality average score was NAP (3.18 ± 0.75), AV (2.81 ± 1.08), and AP (2.59 ± 1.20). Poor ability to make friends average score was NAP (2.81 ± 1.08), AV (2.27 ± 1.13), and AP (1.99 ± 1.19). Lack of social skills average score was NAP (3.28 ± 1.00), AV (2.75 ± 1.20), and AP (2.48 ± 1.42). Poor of bodily attractiveness average score was NAP (3.01 ± 0.82), AV (2.65 ± 1.03), and AP (2.44 ± 1.21).

The total average score was significantly lower in the AP group than in the NAP group. This suggests that an individual who is easily focused on something of interest may also have low feelings of inferiority. An individual with AP may therefore be self-contained an uninterested in the opinions of others. Thus, an individual with AP would not needlessly compare him or herself with others. This could account for why feelings of inferiority are low in those with AP. Furthermore, a person with high feelings of inferiority would be unhappy with oneself because of an unrealistically idealistic image of the self: The larger the gap between the ideal and the real self, the more the dissatisfaction with the real image increases, and feelings of inferiority are born. People with AP are considered to prefer challenges they find a bit difficult. Therefore, it is important to increase opportunities for such challenges in daily life to decrease feelings of inferiority.

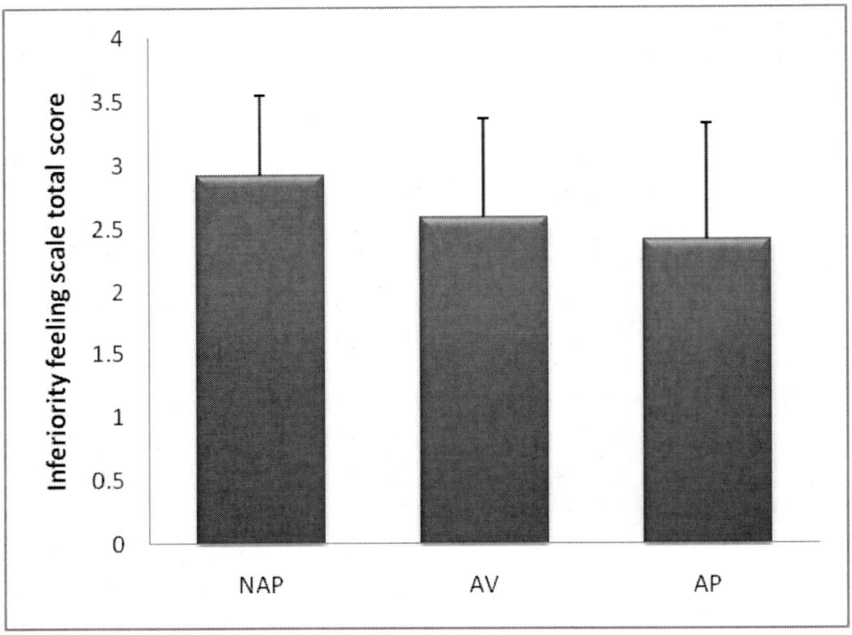

Figure 1. Comparison of the total scores on the Feelings of Inferiority Scale for the three groups.

Figure 2 compares bad personality scores of the three groups. Bad personality scores indicate feelings of inferiority about one's own character (e.g. speaking ill of oneself or considering oneself to say thoughtless things) [9]. Bad personality in the AP group was significantly lower than in the NAP group. Those who speak ill of others do so because feeling like he had stood at the top than the person is caused by that look down on people (i.e. self-defense). People with AP do not need to speak ill of others because they do not feel the need to put themselves above others.

It is thought that AP can determine one's self-image.

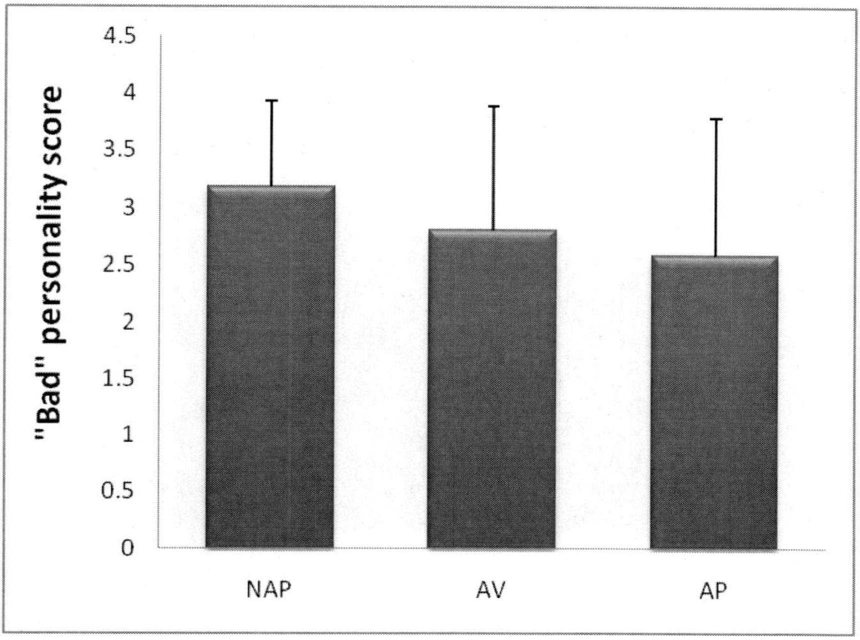

Figure 2. Comparison of bad personality scores in the three groups.

Figure 3 compares the scores for "poor ability to make friends" across the three groups. Scores in the AP group were significantly lower than in the NAP group. The scores reflect the feelings of inferiority resulting from failing to cultivate effective friendships (e.g. not fitting into social groups well and not having many friends) [9]. Many of those with weak friendship bonds are easily hurt and lack self-confidence, and thus, turn to others for their evaluations of oneself. A person with AP, on the other hand, has developed internal values as a point of reference and is not hurt as much by rejection. Thus, they can confidently join social groups.

Figure 4 compares the scores for lack of social skills in the three groups. These scores measure feelings of inferiority about a lack of power or leadership ability [9]. Scores in the AP group were significantly lower than those in the NAP group. To demonstrate leadership, one must have the confidence to give orders to others. A person who fears or anticipates rejection of his or her authority cannot demonstrate leadership. A person with AP does not worry about such rejection and is able to act according to personal beliefs.

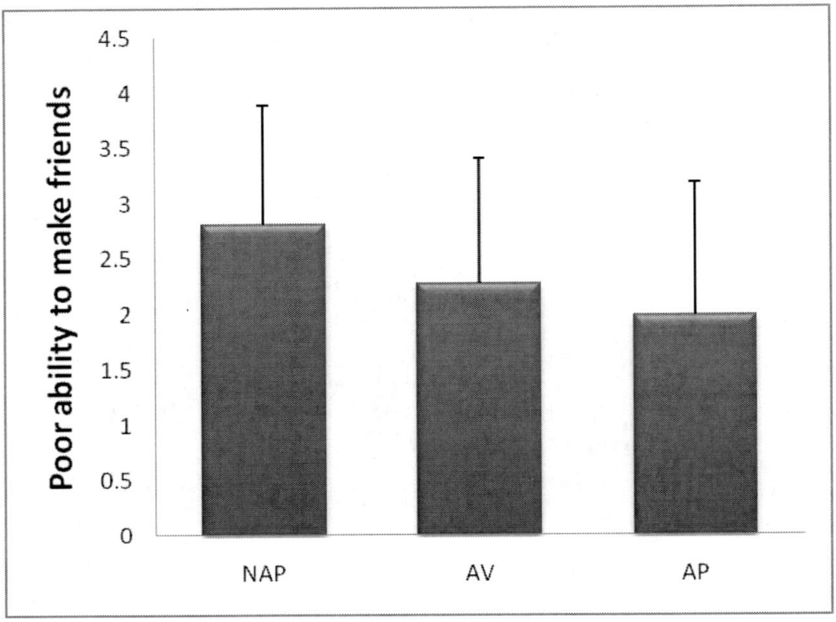

Figure 3. Comparison of poor ability to make friends scores in the three groups.

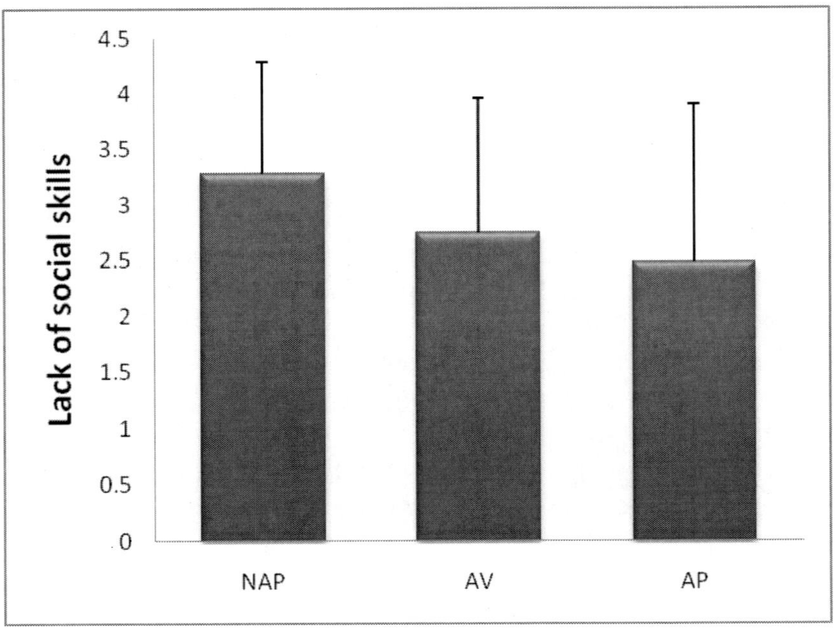

Figure 4. Comparison of scores for lack of social skills in the three groups.

Figure 5 compares the scores for poor perception of bodily attractiveness in the three groups. Poor scores for perceptions of bodily attractiveness reflect feelings of inferiority about one's appearance (such as clothing styles) [9]. Scores in the AP group were significantly lower than those in the NAP group. Young people in particular suffer from feelings of inferiority related to appearance.

Persons with AP, however, are not as dependent on the evaluations of others on their appearance, but rather, judge appearance according to their own evaluation. Therefore, people with AP do not needlessly worry about their appearance.

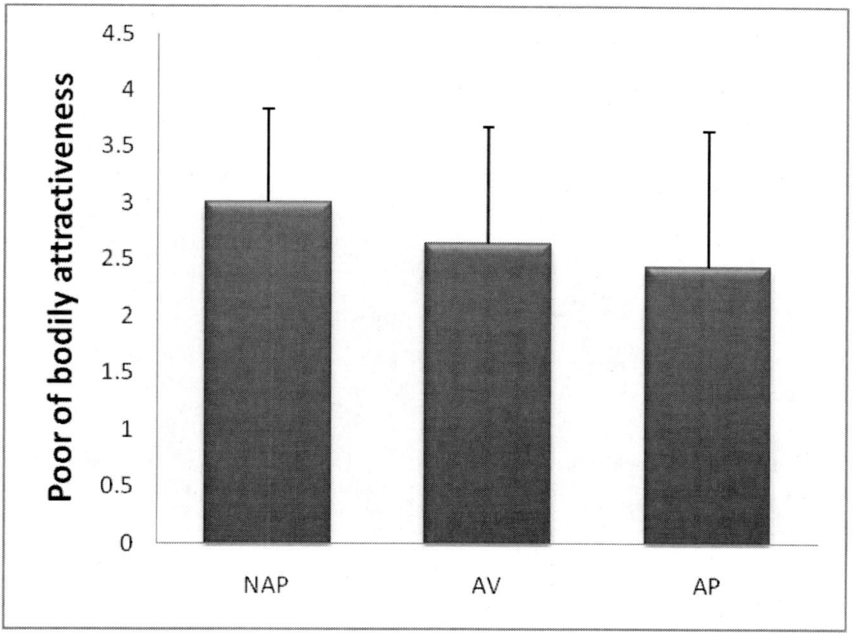

Figure 5. Comparison of scores for poor perceptions of bodily attractiveness in the three groups.

This chapter is based on a study first reported in Hirao K. 2014. Comparison of feelings of inferiority among university students with autotelic, average, and nonautotelic personalities. *N Am J Med Sci*. Sep; 6(9):440–4

References

[1] Nakamura J, Csikszentmihalyi M. 2005. The concept of flow. In: Snyder CR, Lopez SJ, editors. *Handbook of positive psychology*, New York: Oxford University Press; p. 89–105.

[2] Busch H, Hofer J, Chasiotis A, Campos D. 2013. The achievement of flow motive as an element of the autotelic personality: Predicting educational attainment in three cultures. *European Journal of Psychology of Education* 28, Issue 2, pp 239–254.

[3] Tan FB. 2011. Dimensions of Autotelic Personality and their Effects on Perceived Playfulness in the Context of Mobile Information and Entertainment Services. *Australasian Journal of Information Systems* 17:1.

[4] Asakawa K. 2004 Flow experience and autotelic personality in Japanese college students: How do they experience challenges in daily life? *J Happiness Stud.* 5:123–54.

[5] Peterson C, Park N, Seligman ME. 2005 Orientations to happiness and life satisfaction: The full life versus the empty life. *J Happiness Stud.* 6:25–41.

[6] Hirao K. 2014. Comparison of feelings of inferiority among university students with autotelic, average, and nonautotelic personalities. *N Am J Med Sci.* 6(9):440–4.

[7] Ishimura I. 2009. *Psychological study on enhancing factors and positive functions of flow experiences.* Ibaraki: Doctoral thesis from the School of Comprehensive Human Sciences, University of Tsukuba.

[8] Ishimura I, Kodama M. 2009. Flow experiences in everyday activities of Japanese college students: Autotelic people and time management. *Jpn Psychol Res.* 51:47–54.

[9] Kosaka Y. 2008. Developmental changes in inferiority feelings in adolescents and young adults: Important areas of the self. *Jpn J Educ Psychol.* 56:218–29.

[10] Gouva M, Mentis M, Kotrotsiou S, Paralikas T, Kotrotsiou E. 2014. Shame and Anxiety Feelings of a Roma Population in Greece. *J Immigr Minor Health.* [Epub ahead of print] PubMed PMID: 24845934.

[11] Gilbert P, McEwan K, Irons C, Bhundia R, Christie R, Broomhead C, Rockliff H. 2010. Self-harm in a mixed clinical population: The roles of self-criticism, shame, and social rank. *Br J Clin Psychol.* 49(Pt 4): 563–76.

[12] Takahashi H, Tsuji H, Honma M, Shibaki H, Nakamura S, Hashimoto Y, Takahashi M, Koike K, Takei A, Ishida-Yamamoto A, Iizuka H. 2013. Japanese patients with psoriasis and atopic dermatitis show distinct personality profiles. *J Dermatol.* May;40(5):370–3.

[13] Angst J, Gamma A, Rössler W, Ajdacic V, Klein DN. Long-term depression versus episodic major depression: results from the prospective Zurich study of acommunity sample. *J Affect Disord.* 115(1–2):112–21.

[14] Skodlar B, Tomori M, Parnas J. 2008. Subjective experience and suicidal ideation in schizophrenia. *Compr Psychiatry* 49(5):482–8.

[15] Goodwin RD, Marusic A. 2003. Feelings of inferiority and suicide ideation and suicide attempts among youth. *Croat Med J.* (5):553–7.

Chapter 13

Autotelic Personality and Quality of Life

Abstract

This chapter compares health-related QOL in the three groups (autotelic personality (AP), average (AV), or non-autotelic personality (NAP)). I first note that the mental component summary and mental health in the AP group was significantly higher than that in the NAP group. Second, I explain that general health in the AP group was significantly higher than in the NAP group. Third, I show that the vitality of the AP group was significantly higher than that of the NAP group. Fourth, I show that social functioning in the AP group was significantly higher than that in the NAP group. Finally, I show that the scores for role-emotional in the AP group were significantly higher than in the NAP group.

Introduction

Chapter 4 examined the flow experience and quality of life (QOL). In this chapter, I explore the relationships between Autotelic Personality (AP) and QOL. AP is defined as an individual who spends more time in the flow state [1].

The subjects targeted for this chapter covered in this chapter were persons who were unemployed [2]. Participants included job trainees not receiving unemployment benefits from the Emergency training and employment support fund of the Ministry of Health, Labour and Welfare (N = 134). Previous research has suggested that unemployment is associated with spatial health inequalities [3], poor self-rated health [4], mental illness [4], and tobacco consumption [4]. Thus, the unemployed could be considered physically weak.

Comparison of Health-related QOL in the Three Groups (AP, AV, or NAP)

The Flow Experience Checklist was used to diagnose AP [5]. HRQOL were assessed with the Medical Outcome Study 8-Item Short-Form Health Survey (SF-8) [6]. The average age of the participants was 36.14 ± 11.54 year. The $\chi 2$ test and one-way analysis of variance (ANOVA) were performed for the 3 groups (NAP, AV, AP) using the dependent variables of age, gender, SF-8. Tukey's test was used for multiple comparisons.

Based on the mean values (Mean = 1.90) with a margin of ±1 SD (SD = 1.57) of the number of flow activities, 3 groups related to AP characteristics were classified. For the NAP group (n = 30, 22.4%), the number of flow activities was 0. For the average group (n = 82, 61.2%), the number of flow activities was 1–3. For the AP group (n = 22, 16.4%), the number of flow activities was more than 4.

Physical component summary score was NAP (47.3 ± 8.44), AV (48.21 ± 6.30), and AP (49.73 ± 6.6). Mental component summary score was NAP (41.88 ± 8.43), AV (45.44 ± 6.46), and AP (49.48 ± 5.14). Physical functioning score was NAP (47.2 ± 8.4), AV (48.65 ± 8.28), and AP (49.88 ± 5.09). Role physical score was NAP (47.1 ± 5.83), AV (48.98 ± 6.40), and AP (50.88 ± 4.14). Bodily pain score was NAP (47.26 ± 10.29), AV (46.26 ± 8.56), and AP (48.24 ± 9.43). General health perception score was NAP (44.42 ± 8.71), AV (48.67 ± 7.09), and AP (52.56 ± 6.24). Vitality score was NAP (45.56 ± 7.65), AV (49.25 ± 6.34), and AP (53.36 ± 6.17). Social functioning score was NAP (44.26 ± 9.91), AV (47.28 ± 8.04), and AP (50.23 ± 5.84). Role Emotional score was NAP (45.27 ± 6.78), AV (46.67 ± 6.94), and AP (50.74 ± 5.32). Mental health score was NAP (41.85 ± 7.54), AV (45.40 ± 7.55), and AP (48.44 ± 5.52).

Figures 1 and 6 compare the mental component summary (MCS) scores and Comparison of Mental health (MH) scores in the three groups. MCS scores in the AP group were significantly higher than those in the AV or NAP groups, and significantly higher in the AV group than in the NAP group. MH in the AP group was significantly higher than that in the NAP group.

The MCS reflects the mental QOL. Therefore, even if a person with AP is unemployed, he or she will maintain a healthy mental state. AP is thought to exert a deep enough influence to maintain mental health, even during unemployment.

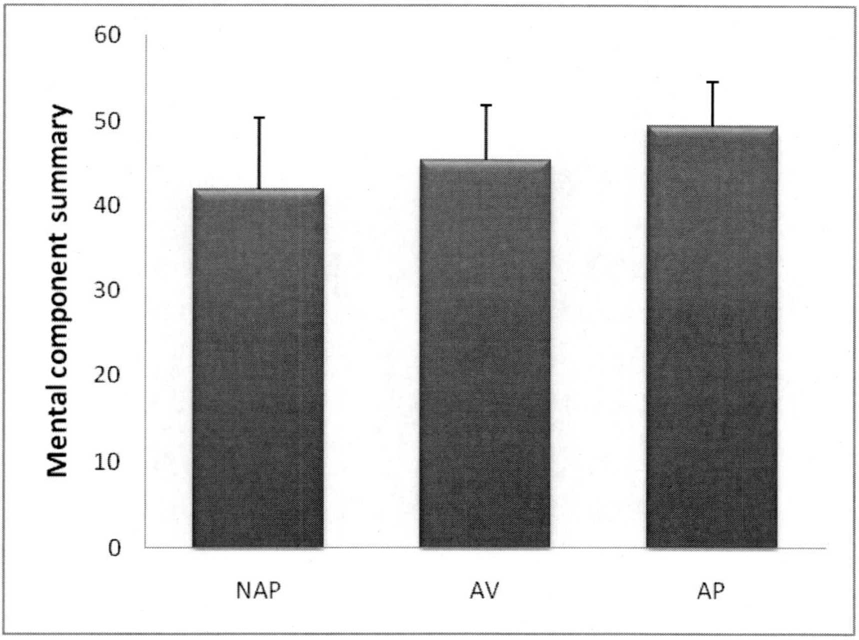

Figure 1. Comparison of mental component summary scores in the three groups.

Figure 2 compares general health (GH) scores in the three groups. These scores represent the overall quality of physical health. GH in the AP group was significantly higher than in the NAP group It is important for an unemployed person to maintain good health to re-enter the job market. AP is an element that can contribute to physical health in the unemployed.

Figure 3 compares vitality (VT) scores in the three groups. VT in the AP group was significantly higher than that in the AV and NAP groups and significantly higher in the AV group than in the NAP group.

Vitality is the necessary energy an unemployed person needs to acquire a job. This is because a person with vitality works productively even if unemployed. In this way, it is closely related to the vitality there are a plurality activities that can be immersed in everyday life.

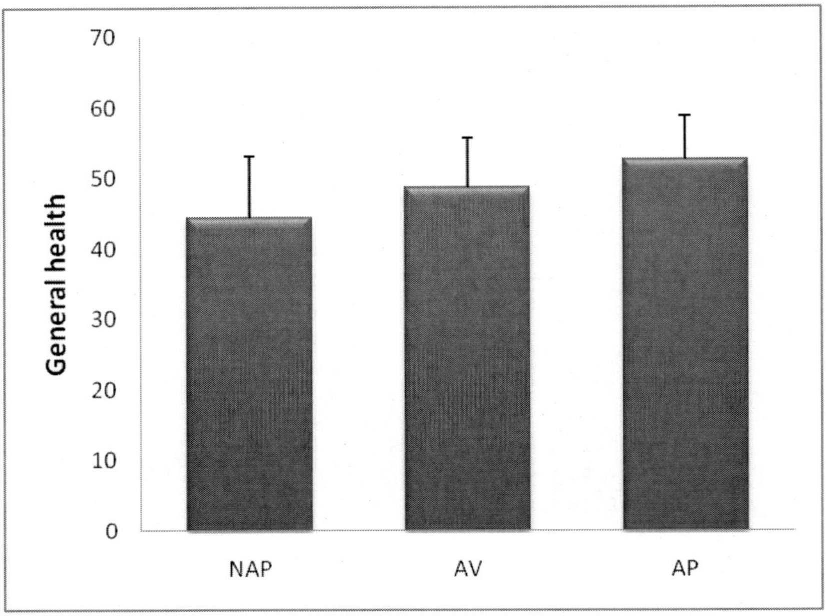

Figure 2. Comparison of general health scores in the three groups.

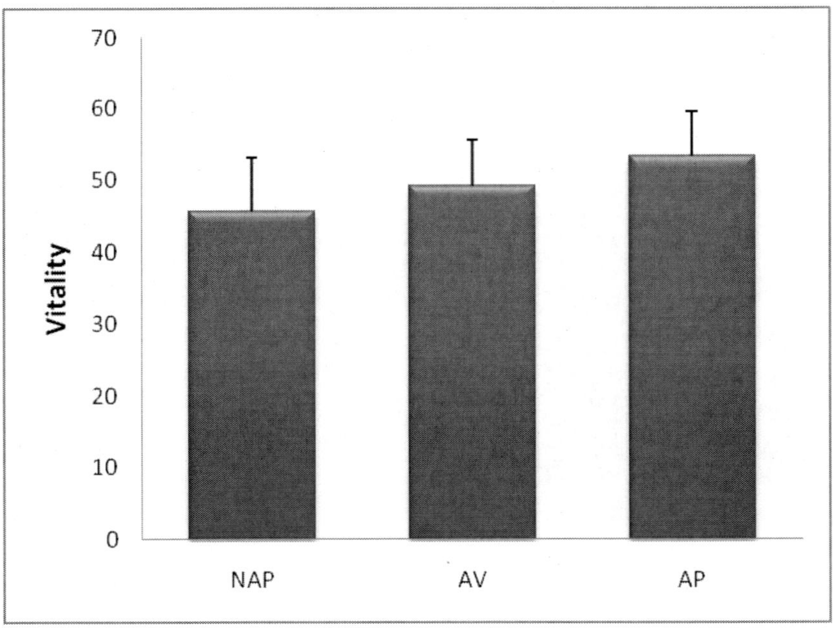

Figure 3. Comparison of vitality scores in the three groups.

Figure 4 compares social functioning (SF) scores in the three groups. SF scores represent the state of one's usual relationship with surrounding people and the degree to which they are impeded by physical or psychological issues. Such relationships are crucial in daily life and can be negatively impacted by unemployment. In particular, financial problems resulting from unemployment impact relationships with family and friends. SF in the AP group was significantly higher than that in the NAP group. This could be because those with AP might be able to interact with others and maintain good health through immersion in multiple activities.

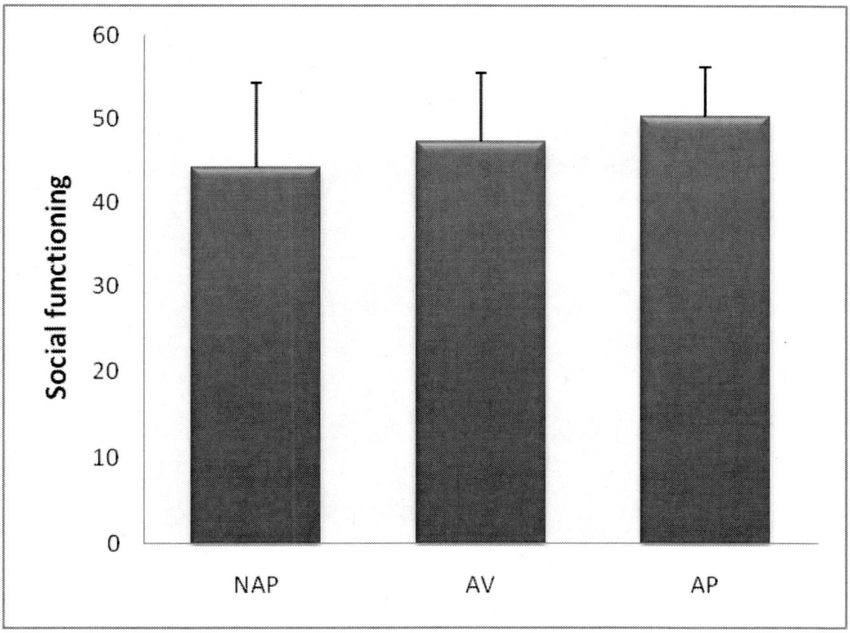

Figure 4. Comparison of social functioning scores in the three groups.

Figure 5 compares role-emotional (RE) scores in the three groups. RE scores reflect the presence or absence of psychological problems related to work and usual activities.

RE scores in the AP group were significantly higher than those in the AV and NAP groups. Because a person with AP can judge things calmly, everyday activities do not cause problems. It is also possible that the psychologically stable base of AP individuals allows them to devote themselves to multiple activities in everyday life.

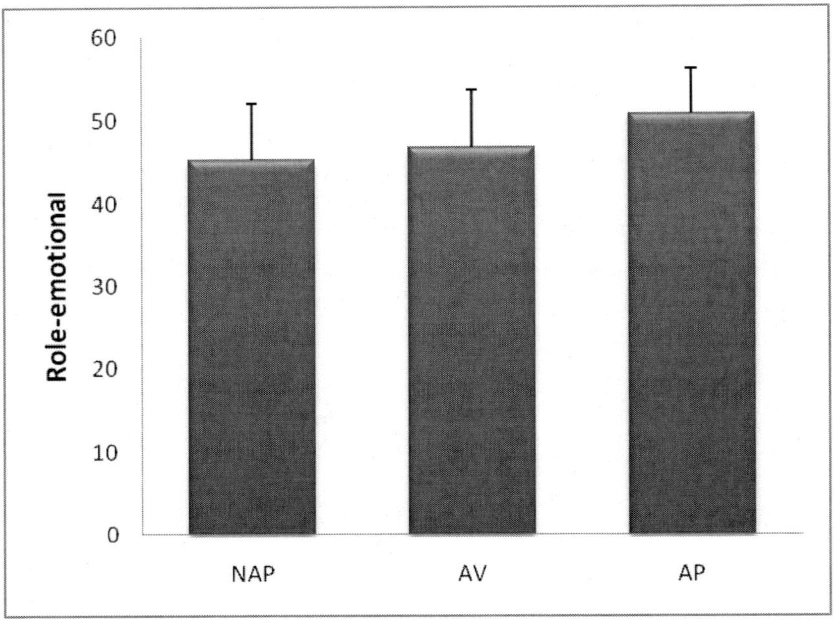

Figure 5. Comparison of role-emotional scores in the three groups.

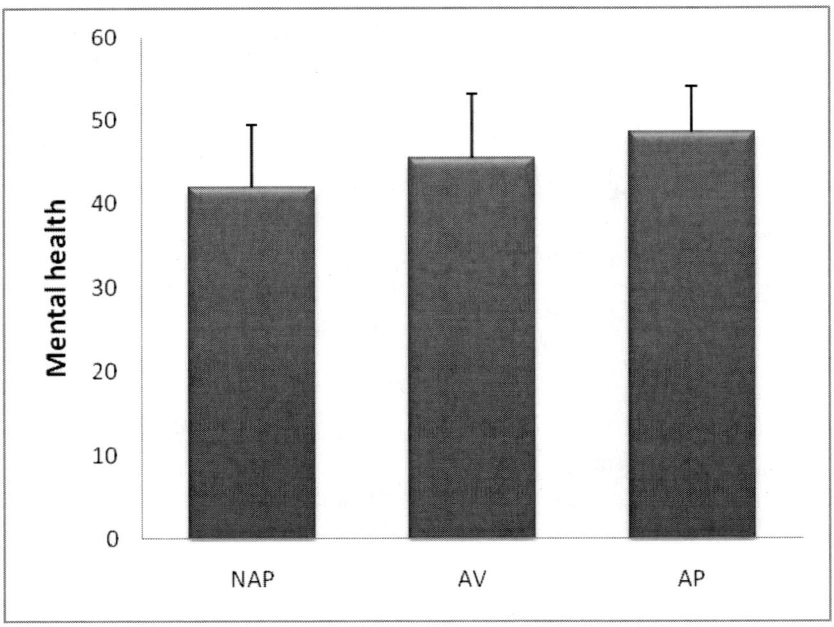

Figure 6. Comparison of mental health scores in the three groups.

This chapter is based on Hirao K, Kobayashi R. 2013. Health-related quality of life and sense of coherence among the unemployed with autotelic, average, and non-autotelic personalities: a cross-sectional survey in Hiroshima, Japan. PLoS One. 8(9):e73915.

References

[1] Nakamura J, Csikszentmihalyi M. 2005. The concept of Flow. In: Snyder CR, Lopez SJ, editors. *Handbook of positive psychology*, New York: Oxford University Press, p. 89–105.

[2] Hirao K, Kobayashi R. 2013. Health-related quality of life and sense of coherence among the unemployed with autotelic, average, and non-autotelic personalities: a cross-sectional survey in Hiroshima, Japan. PLoS One. 8(9):e73915.

[3] Voutilainen A, Hartikainen S, Sherwood PR, Taipale H, Tolppanen AM, Vehviläinen-Julkunen K. 2015. Associations across spatial patterns of disease incidences, socio-demographics, and land use in Finland 1991–2010. *Scand J Public Health*. pii: 1403494815572721. [Epub ahead of print] PubMed PMID:25743878.

[4] Aguilar-Palacio I, Carrera-Lasfuentes P, Rabanaque MJ. 2015. Youth unemployment and economic recession in Spain: Influence on health and lifestyles in young people (16-24 years old). *Int J Public Health*. [Epub ahead of print] PubMed PMID: 25724155.

[5] Ishimura I. 2009. *Psychological study on enhancing factors and positive functions of flow experiences*. Ibaraki: Doctoral thesis from the School of Comprehensive Human Sciences, University of Tsukuba.

[6] Fukuhara S, Suzukamo Y. 2004. *Manual of the SF-8 Japanese version*, Kyoto, Institute for Health Outcomes & Process Evaluation Research.

Chapter 14

Autotelic Personality and Sense of Coherence

Abstract

This chapter compares the sense of coherence in the three previously defined groups (autotelic personality (AP), average (AV), or non-autotelic personality (NAP). First, I provide an overview of sense of coherence. Second, I introduce a method of measuring sense of coherence. Third, I show that a sense of coherence, manageability, meaningfulness, and comprehensibility in the AP group were significantly higher than those in the NAP group.

Sense of Coherence

Sense of coherence (SOC) is a central concept of salutogenesis [1,2]. SOC comprises the following three mechanisms for coping with stressors [3]. First is the ability to understand an event and a problem and predict its outcome [3]. Second is the ability to mobilize stress-coping resources successfully and connect the solution to the problem [3]. Third is the ability to perceive an event positively and arrest a self again [3].

Previous research has suggested that lower SOC is associated with mortality [4], metabolic syndrome and lifestyle [5], and depressive symptoms [6].

Measurement of SOC

The studies described in this chapter used a University of Tokyo Health Sociology version of the SOC3 scale (SOC-3) [7]. SOC-3 contains 3 items (manageability, meaningfulness, and comprehensibility) scored on a 7-point scale. Internal consistency was confirmed by Cronbach's α (0.843). Convergent validity (SOC13) was 0.514, and concurrent validity (Self-Rated Health) was 0.245.

Comparison of Sense of Coherence in the Three Groups (AP, AV, or NAP)

The flow experience checklist was used for the diagnosis of AP [8]. SOC was measured with SOC-3 [7]. Participants were the unemployed people surveyed in Chapter 13 (Average age: 36.14 ± 11.54 year: N = 134).

The $\chi 2$ test and one-way analysis of variance (ANOVA) were performed for the three groups (NAP, AV, AP) using the dependent variables of age, gender, SOC. Tukey's test was used for multiple comparisons.

Based on the mean values (Mean = 1.90) with a margin of ±1 SD (SD = 1.57) of the number of flow activities, three groups related to AP characteristics were classified. For the NAP group (n = 30, 22.4%), the number of flow activities was 0. For the average group (n = 82, 61.2%), the number of flow activities was 1–3. For the AP group (n = 22, 16.4%), the number of flow activities was more than 4.

SOC total score was NAP (11.33 ± 4.35), AV (14.74 ± 3.16), and AP (17 ± 3.15). Manageability score was NAP (3.6 ± 1.5), AV (4.77 ± 1.23), and AP (5.32 ± 1.43). Meaningfulness score was NAP (4.2 ± 1.63), AV (5.51 ± 1.29), and AP (6.18 ± 0.96). Comprehensibility score was NAP (3.53 ± 1.63), AV (4.46 ± 1.34), and AP (5.5 ± 1.34).

Figure 1 compares the total SOC3 scores of the three groups. SOC scores reflect stress-coping ability, health retention capacity, and the willingness to live. The scores in the AP group were significantly higher than those in the AV and NAP groups, and SOC3 in the AV group was significantly higher than that in the NAP group. The AP will say that combines the power to live. Because AP reflects the positive trait of being devoted to something, a person with AP will tend to live positively.

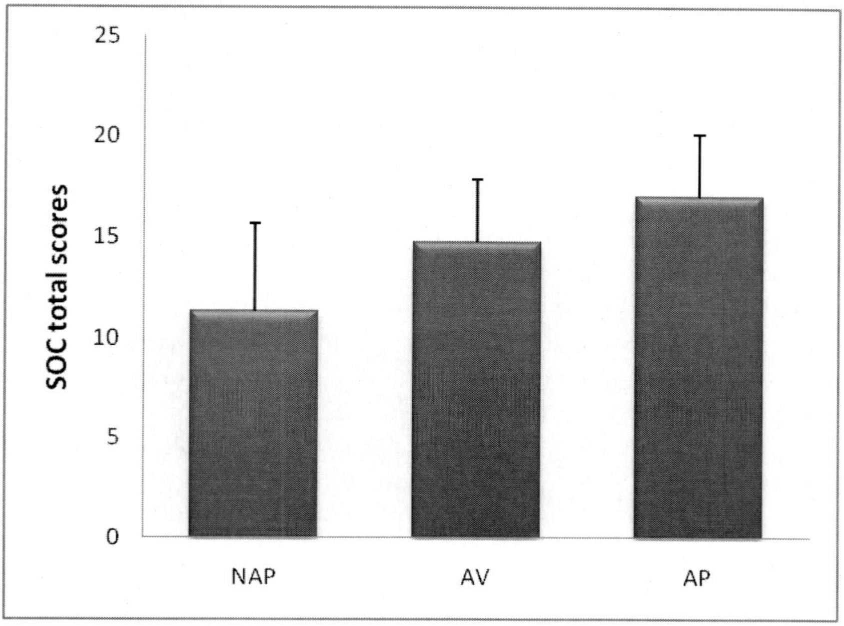

Figure 1. Comparison of the SOC3 scale total scores in the three groups.

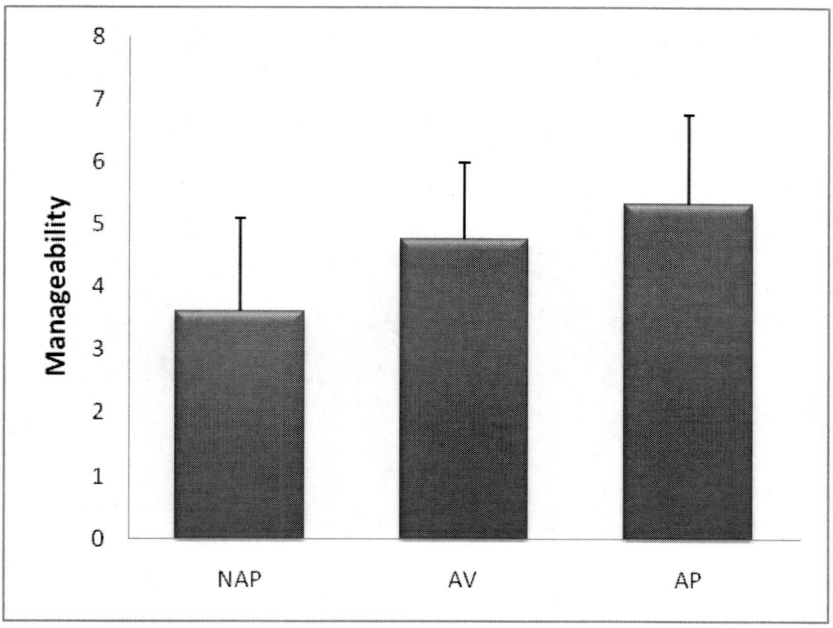

Figure 2. Comparison of manageability scores in the three groups.

Figure 2 compares manageability scores in the three groups. Manageability in the AP group was significantly higher than in NAP group, and it was significantly higher in the AV group than in the NAP group. The manageability score represents one's confidence in coping with difficult situations and represents the feeling of becoming somehow. An individual with AP is likely to have the ability to overcome a difficult situation. Such an ability is highly important for the unemployed.

Figure 3 compares meaningfulness scores in the three groups. Meaningfulness is expressed relative to one's own life and encompasses the feeling that blessed the values at the same time. Meaningfulness in the AP group was significantly higher than that in the NAP group, and it was significantly higher in the AV group than in the NAP group.

Because people with AP could be dedicated to multiple activities, they may have many reasons to find value in their own lives.

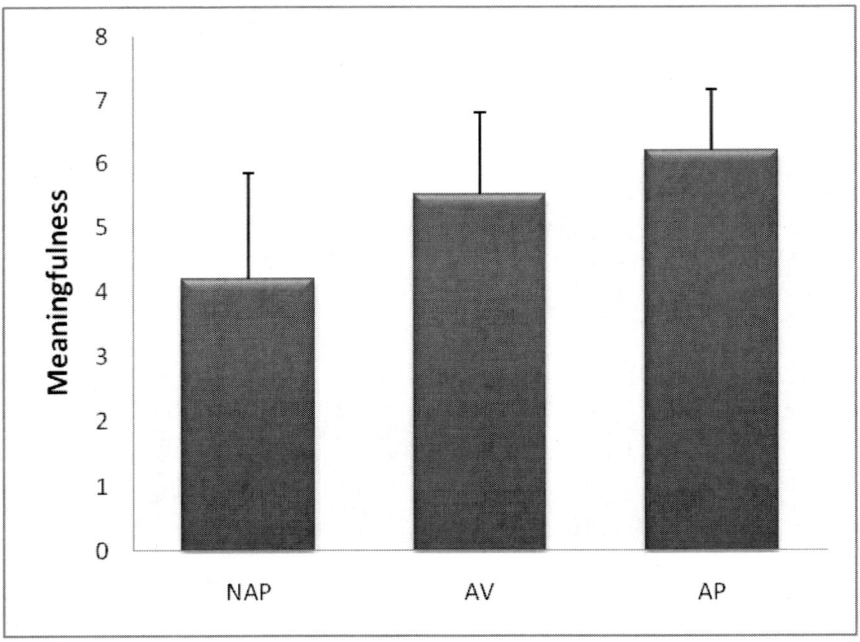

Figure 3. Comparison of meaningfulness scores in the three groups.

Figure 4 compares comprehensibility scores across the three groups. Comprehensibility was significantly higher in the AP group than in the AV and NAP groups, and it was significantly higher in the AV group than in the NAP group. Comprehensibility is predicted and conditions which they are located, a situation that would occur to some extent the future, represents a sense that can be understood. Thus, it is a necessary trait for survival. It is thought that AP is good at a sense to foresee a point.

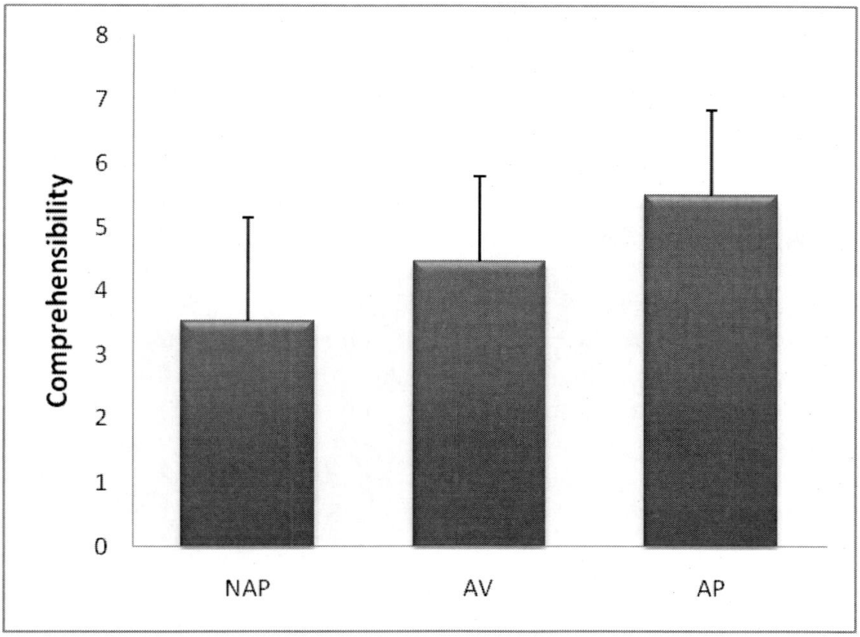

Figure 4. Comparison of comprehensibility scores in the three groups.

This chapter is based on Hirao K, Kobayashi R. 2013. Health-related quality of life and sense of coherence among the unemployed with autotelic, average, and non-autotelic personalities: A cross-sectional survey in Hiroshima, Japan. PLoS One 8(9):e73915

References

[1] Kickbush I. 1996. Tribute to Aaron Antonovsky- What creates health?. *Health Promotion International* 11:5–6.

[2] Eriksson M, Lindström B. 2008 A salutogenic interpretation of the Ottawa Charter. *Health Promotion International* 23:190–199.

[3] Antonovsky, A. 1987. *Unraveling the mystery of health: How people manage stress and stay well.* San Francisco: Jossey-Bass Publishers.

[4] Geulayov G, Drory Y, Novikov I, Dankner R. 2014. Sense of coherence and 22-year all-cause mortality in adult men. *J Psychosom Res*. pii:S0022-3999(14)00446-2. doi: 10.1016/j.jpsychores.2014.12.010. [Epub ahead of print] PubMed PMID: 25637524.

[5] Morita Y, Ohta M, Inoue T, Honda T, Konno Y, Eguchi Y, Yamato H. 2014. Sense of coherence is significantly associated with both metabolic syndrome and lifestyle in Japanese computer software office workers. *Int J Occup Med Environ Health* 27(6):967–79.

[6] Ngai FW, Ngu SF. 2015. Predictors of maternal and paternal depressive symptoms at postpartum. *J Psychosom Res*. 78(2):156–61.

[7] Togari T, Yamazaki Y, Nakayama K, Shimizu J. 2007. Development of a short version of the sense of coherence scale for population survey. *J Epidemiol Community Health* 61: 921–922.

[8] Ishimura I. 2009. *Psychological study on enhancing factors and positive functions of flow experiences*. Ibaraki: Doctoral thesis from the School of Comprehensive Human Sciences, University of Tsukuba.

Author's Contact Information

Dr.Kazuki Hirao, PhD, OTR
Assistant Professor
Department of Occupational Therapy,
School of Health Science and Social Welfare,
Kibi International University
8 Iga-Machi, Takahashi, Okayama 716-8508, Japan
Fax No: +81-866-22-4044
Email: hirao-k@kiui.ac.jp

Index

N

O

P